Contents

Page 78

Page 118

Page 142

Page 206

NESTLÉ® TOLL HOUSE®
Celebrates Baking Magic

In 1930, Kenneth and Ruth Wakefield purchased a Cape Cod-style Toll House located on the outskirts of Whitman, Massachussets. The house served as a haven for road-weary travelers, and was over 200 years old when the Wakefields decided to open it as Toll House Inn.

In keeping with the tradition of creating delicious homemade meals, Ruth baked for the guests.

One day while preparing a batch of Butter Drop Do cookies, a favorite recipe dating back to Colonial days, Ruth cut a bar of Nestlé Semi-Sweet Chocolate into tiny bits and added them to her dough expecting them to melt. Instead, the chocolate held its shape and softened to a delicately creamy texture. The Toll House cookie was born!

Since they were first used by Ruth Wakefield in what would become an extremely popular cookie, Nestlé Toll House Semi-Sweet Morsels have satisfied the chocolate cravings of millions. Today, they're used to make many of the hundreds of delectable chocolate desserts all around the globe.

There are a million reasons to bake with Nestlé Toll House. For these recipes, and others featuring Nestlé Carnation® Milks and Libby's® Pumpkin, visit VeryBestBaking.com.

Original NESTLÉ® TOLL HOUSE®
Chocolate Chip Cookies

Makes about 5 dozen cookies

2¼ **cups all-purpose flour**

1 **teaspoon baking soda**

1 **teaspoon salt**

1 **cup (2 sticks) butter, softened**

¾ **cup granulated sugar**

¾ **cup packed brown sugar**

1 **teaspoon vanilla extract**

2 **large eggs**

2 **cups (12-ounce package) NESTLÉ® TOLL HOUSE® Semi-Sweet Chocolate Morsels**

1 **cup chopped nuts**

PREHEAT oven to 375° F.

COMBINE flour, baking soda and salt in small bowl. Beat butter, granulated sugar, brown sugar and vanilla extract in large mixer bowl until creamy. Add eggs, one at a time, beating well after each addition. Gradually beat in flour mixture. Stir in morsels and nuts. Drop by rounded tablespoon onto ungreased baking sheets.

BAKE for 9 to 11 minutes or until golden brown. Cool on baking sheets for 2 minutes; remove to wire racks to cool completely.

Pan Cookie Variation:

GREASE *15×10-inch jelly-roll pan. Prepare dough as above. Spread in prepared pan. Bake for 20 to 25 minutes or until golden brown. Cool in pan on wire rack. Makes 4 dozen bars.*

Prep Time: 15 minutes
Baking Time: 9 minutes

All-Time
NESTLÉ Favorites

Become one of the Very Best Bakers with these tried-and-true
recipes. From cookies and pies, to brownies and cakes,
you'll find enticing baked goods to please any palate.
You're guaranteed to satisfy your sweet tooth.

Chunky Milk Chocolate Chip Cookies

Makes about 2½ dozen cookies

2 cups all-purpose flour

1 teaspoon baking soda

¼ teaspoon salt

1¼ cups packed brown sugar

1 cup (2 sticks) butter or
   margarine, softened

1 teaspoon vanilla extract

1 large egg

1¾ cups (11.5-ounce package)
   NESTLÉ® TOLL HOUSE® Milk
   Chocolate Morsels

1 cup chopped nuts

1 cup raisins

PREHEAT oven to 375° F.

COMBINE flour, baking soda and salt in small bowl. Beat
sugar, butter and vanilla extract in large mixer bowl until
creamy. Beat in egg. Gradually beat in flour mixture. Stir in
morsels, nuts and raisins. Drop by heaping tablespoon onto
ungreased baking sheets; flatten slightly.

BAKE for 9 to 11 minutes or until edges are lightly browned.
Cool on baking sheets for 2 minutes; remove to wire racks
to cool completely.

The Ultimate NESTLÉ® TOLL HOUSE® Chocolate Cake

Makes 12 servings

CAKE

- 1½ cups granulated sugar
- 1½ cups all-purpose flour
- ¾ teaspoon baking soda
- ½ teaspoon salt
- 1 cup strong coffee
- 1½ bars (6 ounces) NESTLÉ® TOLL HOUSE® Dark Chocolate Baking Bar
- ½ cup vegetable oil
- ½ cup sour cream, room temperature
- 2 large eggs, room temperature
- 1½ teaspoons vanilla extract

FROSTING

- ⅔ cup heavy whipping cream
- 5 tablespoons unsalted butter, cut into ½-inch pieces
- 3 tablespoons granulated sugar
- 3 tablespoons water
- ⅛ teaspoon salt
- 2½ bars (10 ounces) NESTLÉ® TOLL HOUSE® Dark Chocolate Baking Bar, finely chopped
- ½ teaspoon vanilla extract

FOR CAKE

PREHEAT oven to 350° F. Grease two 8-inch-round cake pans. Line bottoms with wax paper.

COMBINE sugar, flour, baking soda and salt in large bowl. Bring coffee to simmer in small, *heavy-duty* saucepan. Remove from heat. Add chocolate; whisk until chocolate is melted and smooth. Cool slightly.

WHISK vegetable oil, sour cream, eggs and vanilla extract in another large bowl to blend. Add chocolate-coffee mixture; whisk to blend well. Add *one-third* of chocolate-sour cream mixture to dry ingredients; whisk to blend well. Add *remaining* chocolate-sour cream mixture in two more additions, whisking well after each addition. Divide batter equally between prepared pans. (Batter will be thin.)

BAKE for 33 to 35 minutes or until wooden pick inserted in centers comes out clean. Cool in pans on wire racks for 10 minutes. Run knife around edges of cakes. Invert onto wire racks; remove wax paper. Cool completely. Spread frosting between layers and over top and sides of cake. Store any leftover cake in refrigerator. Bring to room temperature before serving.

FOR FROSTING

BRING cream, butter, sugar, water and salt to simmer in medium, *heavy-duty* saucepan over medium heat, stirring frequently. Remove from heat. Immediately add chocolate; let stand for 2 minutes. Whisk until melted and smooth. Add vanilla extract. Pour into medium bowl. Refrigerate, stirring occasionally, for about 1½ hours or until thick enough to spread.

Oatmeal Scotchies

Makes about 4 dozen cookies

1¼ cups all-purpose flour

1 teaspoon baking soda

½ teaspoon salt

½ teaspoon ground cinnamon

1 cup (2 sticks) butter or margarine, softened

¾ cup granulated sugar

¾ cup packed brown sugar

2 large eggs

1 teaspoon vanilla extract or grated peel of 1 orange

3 cups quick or old-fashioned oats

1⅔ cups (11-ounce package) NESTLÉ® TOLL HOUSE® Butterscotch Flavored Morsels

PREHEAT oven to 375° F.

COMBINE flour, baking soda, salt and cinnamon in small bowl. Beat butter, granulated sugar, brown sugar, eggs and vanilla extract in large mixer bowl. Gradually beat in flour mixture. Stir in oats and morsels. Drop by rounded tablespoon onto ungreased baking sheets.

BAKE for 7 to 8 minutes for chewy cookies or 9 to 10 minutes for crispy cookies. Cool on baking sheets for 2 minutes; remove to wire racks to cool completely.

Pan Cookie Variation:

Grease 15×10-inch jelly-roll pan. Prepare dough as above. Spread into prepared pan. Bake for 18 to 22 minutes or until light brown. Cool completely in pan on wire rack. Makes 4 dozen bars.

NESTLÉ® Very Best Fudge

Makes 4 dozen servings
(2 pieces per serving)

3 cups granulated sugar

1 can (12 fluid ounces) NESTLÉ® CARNATION® Evaporated Milk

¼ cup (½ stick) butter or margarine

½ teaspoon salt

4 cups miniature marshmallows

4 cups (24 ounces) or two 12-ounce packages NESTLÉ® TOLL HOUSE® Semi-Sweet Chocolate Morsels

1 cup chopped pecans or walnuts (optional)

2 teaspoons vanilla extract

LINE 13×9-inch baking pan or two 8-inch-square baking pans with foil.

COMBINE sugar, evaporated milk, butter and salt in 4- to 5-quart heavy-duty saucepan. Bring to a *full rolling boil* over medium heat, stirring constantly. Boil, stirring constantly, for 4 to 5 minutes. Remove from heat.

STIR in marshmallows, morsels, nuts, if desired, and vanilla extract. Stir vigorously for 1 minute or until marshmallows are melted. Pour into prepared pan(s). Refrigerate for 2 hours or until firm. Lift from pan; remove foil. Cut into pieces. Store tightly covered in refrigerator. Makes about 4 pounds.

For Milk Chocolate Fudge:

SUBSTITUTE 3½ cups (23 ounces) or 2 packages (11.5 ounces each) NESTLÉ® TOLL HOUSE® Milk Chocolate Morsels for Semi-Sweet Chocolate Morsels.

For Butterscotch Fudge:

SUBSTITUTE 3⅓ cups (22 ounces) or 2 packages (11 ounces each) NESTLÉ® TOLL HOUSE® Butterscotch Flavored Morsels for Semi-Sweet Chocolate Morsels.

For Peanutty Fudge:

SUBSTITUTE 3⅓ cups (22 ounces) or 2 packages (11 ounces each) NESTLÉ® TOLL HOUSE® Peanut Butter & Milk Chocolate Morsels for Semi-Sweet Chocolate Morsels and ½ cup chopped peanuts for pecans or walnuts.

Double Chocolate Chunk Cookies

Makes about 40 cookies

2 cups all-purpose flour

¾ cup NESTLÉ® TOLL HOUSE® Baking Cocoa

1 teaspoon baking soda

½ teaspoon salt

1 cup (2 sticks) butter or margarine, softened

⅔ cup granulated sugar

⅔ cup packed brown sugar

1 teaspoon vanilla extract

2 large eggs

1¾ cups (11.5-ounce package) NESTLÉ® TOLL HOUSE® Semi-Sweet Chocolate Chunks

PREHEAT oven to 350° F.

COMBINE flour, cocoa, baking soda and salt in medium bowl. Beat butter, granulated sugar, brown sugar and vanilla extract in large mixer bowl until creamy. Add eggs, one at a time, beating well after each addition. Gradually beat in flour mixture. Stir in chunks. Drop by rounded tablespoon onto ungreased baking sheets.

BAKE for 9 to 11 minutes or until cookies are puffed and centers are set but still soft. Cool on baking sheets for 2 minutes; remove to wire racks to cool completely.

NESTLÉ® TOLL HOUSE® Chocolate Chip Pie

Makes 8 servings

1 *unbaked* 9-inch (4-cup volume) deep-dish pie shell*

2 large eggs

½ cup all-purpose flour

½ cup granulated sugar

½ cup packed brown sugar

¾ cup (1½ sticks) butter, softened

1 cup (6 ounces) NESTLÉ® TOLL HOUSE® Semi-Sweet Chocolate Morsels

1 cup chopped nuts

Sweetened whipped cream or ice cream (optional)

If using frozen pie shell, use deep-dish style, thawed completely. Bake on baking sheet; increase baking time slightly.

PREHEAT oven to 325° F.

BEAT eggs in large mixer bowl on high speed until foamy. Beat in flour, granulated sugar and brown sugar. Beat in butter. Stir in morsels and nuts. Spoon into pie shell.

BAKE for 55 to 60 minutes or until knife inserted halfway between edge and center comes out clean. Cool on wire rack. Serve warm with whipped cream, if desired.

Zesty Lemon Pound Cake

Makes 12 to 16 servings

1   cup (6 ounces) NESTLÉ®
    TOLL HOUSE® Premier
    White Morsels

2½ cups all-purpose flour

1   teaspoon baking powder

½   teaspoon salt

1   cup (2 sticks) butter, softened

1½ cups granulated sugar

2   teaspoons vanilla extract

3   large eggs

3   to 4 tablespoons grated
    lemon peel (about
    3 medium lemons)

1⅓ cups buttermilk

1   cup powdered sugar

3   tablespoons fresh lemon
    juice

PREHEAT oven to 350° F. Grease and flour 10-cup Bundt pan.

MELT morsels in medium, uncovered, microwave-safe bowl on MEDIUM–HIGH (70%) power for 1 minute; STIR. Morsels may retain some of their original shape. If necessary, microwave at additional 10- to 15-second intervals, stirring just until morsels are melted. Cool slightly.

COMBINE flour, baking powder and salt in small bowl. Beat butter, sugar and vanilla extract in large mixer bowl until creamy. Beat in eggs, one at a time, beating well after each addition. Beat in lemon peel and melted morsels. Gradually beat in flour mixture alternately with buttermilk. Pour into prepared Bundt pan.

BAKE for 50 to 55 minutes or until wooden pick inserted in cake comes out clean. Cool in pan on wire rack for 10 minutes. Combine powdered sugar and lemon juice in small bowl. Make holes in cake with wooden pick; pour *half* of lemon glaze over cake. Let stand for 5 minutes. Invert onto plate. Make holes in top of cake; pour *remaining* glaze over cake. Cool completely before serving.

Gourmet Chocolate Chip Cookies

Makes 4 dozen cookies

2 cups all-purpose flour

¾ cup ground pecans

1 teaspoon baking powder

½ teaspoon baking soda

¼ teaspoon salt

½ cup (1 stick) butter, softened

½ cup vegetable shortening

¾ cup granulated sugar

¾ cup packed brown sugar

2 large eggs

1 teaspoon vanilla extract

1¾ cups (11.5-ounce package)
    NESTLÉ® TOLL HOUSE® Milk
    Chocolate Morsels

1 cup chopped pecans

PREHEAT oven to 375° F.

COMBINE flour, ground pecans, baking powder, baking soda and salt in medium bowl. Beat butter and vegetable shortening in large mixer bowl on medium speed for 30 seconds. Add granulated sugar, brown sugar, eggs and vanilla extract; beat until well combined. Gradually beat in as much flour mixture as possible. Stir in *remaining* flour mixture, morsels and nuts. (Recipe may be made ahead up to this point. If desired, cover and refrigerate dough for 4 hours or up to 3 days.) Drop by rounded teaspoon onto ungreased baking sheets.

BAKE for 10 minutes or until golden brown. Cool on baking sheets for 2 minutes; remove to wire racks to cool completely.

NESTLÉ® TOLL HOUSE® Grand Chocolate Brownie Wedges with Chocolate Sauce

Makes 12 servings

3 **bars (12 ounces) NESTLÉ® TOLL HOUSE® Dark Chocolate Baking Bar,** *divided*

1 **cup granulated sugar**

⅓ **cup butter, cut into pieces**

2 **tablespoons water**

2 **large eggs**

1 **teaspoon vanilla extract**

¾ **cup all-purpose flour**

¼ **teaspoon salt**

½ **cup chopped walnuts or pecans (optional)**

⅓ **cup heavy whipping cream**

Whipped cream (optional)

PREHEAT oven to 325° F. Line 8-inch-square baking pan with foil; grease.

HEAT *10 ounces (2½ bars)* chocolate (broken into small pieces), sugar, butter and water in small, *heavy-duty* saucepan over low heat, stirring constantly, until chocolate and butter are melted. Pour into medium bowl. Stir in eggs, one at a time, until mixed in. Stir in vanilla extract. Add flour and salt; stir well. Stir in nuts, if desired. Pour into prepared baking pan.

BAKE for 35 to 40 minutes or until wooden pick inserted in center comes out slightly sticky (may be up to 45 minutes). Cool in pan on wire rack. Lift brownie from pan with foil to cutting board. Carefully remove foil. Cut brownie square in half. Cut each half into thirds, for a total of 6 pieces. Cut each piece in half diagonally to form triangles for a total of 12.

PLACE cream in small, uncovered, microwave-safe dish. Microwave on HIGH (100%) power for 25 to 30 seconds. Add *remaining 2 ounces (½ bar)* chocolate, broken into small pieces; stir until smooth. (Sauce will thicken as it cools.) Place wedge on serving plate; top or drizzle with a teaspoon of sauce. Top with whipped cream, if desired.

Chocolate Caramel Brownies

Makes 2 dozen brownies

1 **package (15.25 or 18.25 ounces) chocolate cake mix**

1 **cup chopped nuts**

1 **cup NESTLÉ® CARNATION® Evaporated Milk, *divided***

½ **cup (1 stick) butter or margarine, melted**

35 **(10-ounce package) caramels, unwrapped**

2 **cups (12-ounce package) NESTLÉ® TOLL HOUSE® Semi-Sweet Chocolate Morsels**

PREHEAT oven to 350° F.

COMBINE cake mix and nuts in large bowl. Stir in ⅔ *cup* evaporated milk and butter (batter will be thick). Spread *half* of batter into ungreased 13×9-inch baking pan.

BAKE for 15 minutes.

HEAT caramels and *remaining* evaporated milk in small saucepan over low heat, stirring constantly, until caramels are melted. Sprinkle morsels over brownie; drizzle with caramel mixture.

DROP *remaining* batter by heaping teaspoon over caramel mixture.

BAKE for 25 to 30 minutes or until center is set. Cool in pan on wire rack. Cut into 24 squares.

Chocolate Turtle Brownies

Makes 2 dozen brownies

2 cups (12-ounce package) **NESTLÉ® TOLL HOUSE® Semi-Sweet Chocolate Morsels, *divided***

½ cup (1 stick) **butter or margarine, cut into pieces**

3 large **eggs**

1¼ cups **all-purpose flour**

1 cup **granulated sugar**

¼ teaspoon **baking soda**

1 teaspoon **vanilla extract**

½ cup **chopped walnuts**

12 **caramels**

1 tablespoon **milk**

PREHEAT oven to 350° F. Grease 13×9-inch baking pan.

MELT *1 cup* morsels and butter in large, *heavy-duty* saucepan over low heat, stirring constantly until smooth. Remove from heat; stir in eggs. Add flour, sugar, baking soda and vanilla extract; stir well.

SPREAD batter into prepared baking pan; sprinkle with *remaining* morsels and walnuts.

BAKE for 20 to 25 minutes or until wooden pick inserted in center comes out slightly sticky.

MICROWAVE caramels and milk in small, microwave-safe bowl on HIGH (100%) power for 1 minute; STIR. Microwave at additional 10- to 15-second intervals, stirring until melted. Drizzle over warm brownies. Cool in pan on wire rack.

Old-Fashioned Peanut Butter Chocolate Chip Cookies

Makes 3½ dozen cookies

1½ cups all-purpose flour

1 teaspoon baking soda

1 cup (2 sticks) butter or margarine, softened

½ cup creamy or chunky peanut butter

½ cup granulated sugar

½ cup packed brown sugar

1 teaspoon vanilla extract

1 large egg

1¾ cups (11.5-ounce package) NESTLÉ® TOLL HOUSE® Milk Chocolate Morsels

Granulated sugar

PREHEAT oven to 375° F.

COMBINE flour and baking soda in small bowl. Beat butter, peanut butter, granulated sugar, brown sugar and vanilla extract in large mixer bowl until creamy. Beat in egg. Gradually beat in flour mixture. Stir in morsels.

DROP dough by rounded tablespoon onto ungreased baking sheets. Press down slightly with bottom of glass dipped in granulated sugar.

BAKE for 8 to 10 minutes or until edges are set but centers are still soft. Cool on baking sheets for 4 minutes; remove to wire racks to cool completely.

Pan Cookie Variation:

PREPARE dough as above. Spread dough into ungreased 15×10-inch jelly-roll pan. Bake for 15 to 18 minutes. Cool in pan on wire rack.

Triple-Chocolate Cupcakes

Makes 2½ dozen cupcakes

1 **package (15.25 or 18.25 ounces) chocolate cake mix**

1 **package (4 ounces) chocolate instant pudding and pie filling mix**

1 **container (8 ounces) sour cream**

4 **large eggs**

½ **cup vegetable oil**

½ **cup warm water**

2 **cups (12-ounce package) NESTLÉ® TOLL HOUSE® Semi-Sweet Chocolate Morsels**

1 **container (16 ounces) prepared frosting**

Assorted candy sprinkles

PREHEAT oven to 350° F. Grease or paper-line 30 muffin cups.

COMBINE cake mix, pudding mix, sour cream, eggs, vegetable oil and water in large mixer bowl; beat on low speed just until blended. Beat on high speed for 2 minutes. Stir in morsels. Pour into prepared muffin cups, filling ⅔ full.

BAKE for 25 to 28 minutes or until wooden pick inserted in centers comes out clean. Cool in pans for 10 minutes; remove to wire racks to cool completely. Frost; decorate with candy sprinkles.

Molten Chocolate Cakes

2 tablespoons plus ¾ cup (1½ sticks) butter, *divided*

2 bars (8 ounces) NESTLÉ® TOLL HOUSE® Dark Chocolate Baking Bar, broken into pieces

3 large eggs

3 large egg yolks

¼ cup plus 1 tablespoon granulated sugar

1 teaspoon vanilla extract

1 tablespoon all-purpose flour

Powdered sugar

PREHEAT oven to 425° F. Generously butter six (6-ounce) ramekins or custard cups with *2 tablespoons* butter.

STIR *¾ cup* butter and chocolate in medium, *heavy-duty* saucepan over low heat until chocolate is melted and mixture is smooth. Remove from heat. Beat eggs, egg yolks, sugar and vanilla extract in large mixer bowl until thick and pale yellow, about 8 minutes. Fold ⅓ of chocolate mixture into egg mixture. Fold in *remaining* chocolate mixture and flour until well blended. Divide batter evenly among prepared ramekins. Place on baking sheet.

BAKE for 12 to 13 minutes or until sides are set and 1-inch centers move slightly when shaken. Remove from oven to wire rack.

TO SERVE, run a thin knife around top edge of cakes to loosen slightly; carefully invert onto serving plates. Lift ramekins off of cakes. Sprinkle with powdered sugar. Serve immediately.

Quick & Easy Creations

Create delicious desserts and chocolatey snacks even when you're short on time! Whip up bars, bites, beverages, candies, and other tasty treats without the hassle using these easy-to-follow recipes.

Super-Easy Rocky Road Fudge

Makes 4 dozen pieces

- **2 cups (12-ounce package) NESTLÉ® TOLL HOUSE® Semi-Sweet Chocolate Morsels**
- **1 can (14 ounces) NESTLÉ® CARNATION® Sweetened Condensed Milk**
- **1 teaspoon vanilla extract**
- **3 cups miniature marshmallows**
- **1½ cups coarsely chopped walnuts**

LINE 13×9-inch baking pan with foil; grease lightly.

MICROWAVE morsels and sweetened condensed milk in large, uncovered, microwave-safe bowl on HIGH (100%) power for 1 minute; STIR. Morsels may retain some of their original shape. If necessary, microwave at additional 10- to 15-second intervals, stirring just until morsels are melted. Stir in vanilla extract. Fold in marshmallows and nuts.

PRESS mixture into prepared baking pan. Refrigerate until ready to serve. Lift from pan; remove foil. Cut into pieces.

No-Bake Butterscotch Snack Bites

3 cups toasted rice cereal

1 cup quick oats

1 cup coarsely chopped
    walnuts, pecans and/or
    almonds

1⅔ cups (11-ounce package)
    NESTLÉ® TOLL HOUSE®
    Butterscotch Flavored
    Morsels, *divided*

½ teaspoon salt

½ cup light corn syrup

PAPER-LINE or lightly grease 24 muffin cups.

COMBINE cereal, oats, nuts, ½ *cup* morsels and salt in large mixing bowl.

MELT *remaining* morsels and corn syrup in uncovered, microwave-safe bowl on MEDIUM-HIGH (70%) power for 1 minute; STIR. Morsels may retain some of their original shape. If necessary, microwave at additional 10- to 15-second intervals, stirring just until morsels are melted.

DRIZZLE melted morsel mixture over cereal mixture; stir until combined. *Working quickly*, press ¼ cup of mixture into each prepared cup. Let stand at room temperature for 20 minutes or until firm. Store in tightly covered container(s) at room temperature.

For Mini Snack Bites: Paper-line or grease mini muffin cups. Prepare recipe as above; press about 1 tablespoon of mixture into each prepared cup. Makes about 4½ dozen mini snack bites.

For Snack Bite Bars: Lightly grease 13×9-inch baking pan. Prepare recipe as above and press mixture into prepared pan. Let stand at room temperature for 30 minutes or until firm. Makes 2 dozen bars.

Tip:

Morsels can also be melted on top of a double boiler following package melting directions, adding corn syrup to melted morsels.

Nutty Dark Hot Chocolate

Makes 2 servings

2 **cups 1% milk**

½ **cup NESTLÉ® TOLL HOUSE® Dark Chocolate Morsels**

1 **tablespoon reduced-fat creamy peanut butter**

¼ **teaspoon vanilla extract**

HEAT milk, morsels and peanut butter in small saucepan over medium-low heat, stirring frequently, until hot and morsels are melted (do not boil). Stir in vanilla extract. Pour into mugs.

Magic Mint Chocolate Bark

Makes 9 servings
(¾ pound bark)

1⅔ cups (10-ounce package)
   NESTLÉ® TOLL HOUSE®
   Dark Chocolate & Mint
   Morsels

⅓ cup coarsely chopped oven
   roasted or toasted almonds

PREHEAT oven to 325° F. Line small baking sheet with foil or parchment paper.

POUR morsels onto prepared baking sheet. Arrange morsels so they are touching each other in a single layer (roughly an 11×9-inch rectangle).

BAKE for 1 to 3 minutes or until morsels are shiny. Morsels will retain their shape. Remove from oven to wire rack. With tip of butter knife or wooden pick, immediately swirl morsels to create a swirled pattern.

SPRINKLE with nuts. Hold baking sheet 3 inches above counter and drop to settle nuts into melted morsels. Refrigerate for 1 hour or until firm. Break into pieces. Store in airtight container in refrigerator.

Variation:

Substitute broken pretzel pieces or another nut of choice for the almonds.

Easy Toffee Candy

1¼ cups (2½ sticks) butter, *divided*

35 to 40 soda crackers

1 cup packed dark brown sugar

1 can (14 ounces) NESTLÉ® CARNATION® Sweetened Condensed Milk

1½ cups (9 ounces) NESTLÉ® TOLL HOUSE® Semi-Sweet Chocolate Morsels

¾ cup finely chopped walnuts

PREHEAT oven to 425° F. Line 15×10-inch jelly-roll pan with *heavy-duty* foil.

MELT *¼ cup (½ stick)* butter in medium saucepan. Pour into prepared jelly-roll pan. Arrange crackers over butter, breaking crackers to fit empty spaces.

MELT *remaining* butter in same saucepan; add sugar. Bring to a boil over medium heat. Reduce heat to low; cook, stirring occasionally, for 2 minutes. Remove from heat; stir in sweetened condensed milk. Pour over crackers.

BAKE for 10 to 12 minutes or until mixture is bubbly and slightly darkened. Remove from oven; cool for 1 minute.

SPRINKLE with morsels. Let stand for 5 minutes or until morsels are shiny; spread evenly. Sprinkle with nuts; press into chocolate. Cool in pan on wire rack for 30 minutes. Refrigerate for about 30 minutes or until chocolate is set. Remove foil; cut into pieces.

Dark Chocolate Peanut Butter Candies

Makes 30 candies

30 **1-inch paper candy liners**

⅓ **cup creamy peanut butter**

¾ **cup sifted powdered sugar**

1 **tablespoon butter, softened**

1⅔ **cups (10-ounce package) NESTLÉ® TOLL HOUSE® Dark Chocolate Morsels**

1 **tablespoon vegetable shortening**

Coarse sea salt

PLACE paper liners on a baking sheet.

COMBINE peanut butter, sugar and butter in small bowl until well blended. If mixture is very soft, mix in an additional tablespoon of sugar. Shape peanut butter mixture into 30 ½- to ¾-inch balls, flattening slightly.

MELT morsels and vegetable shortening in medium, uncovered, microwave-safe bowl on MEDIUM-HIGH (70%) power for 1 minute; STIR. Morsels may retain some of their shape. If necessary, microwave at additional 10- to 15-second intervals, stirring just until melted. Spoon 1 measuring teaspoon of melted morsels into each cup. Place peanut butter filling onto top of melted morsels. Top each with a measuring half teaspoon of melted morsels. Sprinkle with a few grains of sea salt. Refrigerate for 20 minutes or until firm. Store in covered container in refrigerator.

Tip:

To keep melted chocolate warm, place bowl on top of smaller bowl filled with very warm water. Do not allow water to touch bottom of bowl or allow water to get into chocolate.

Tiny Chocolate Cakes and Fruit Kabobs

Makes 8 servings

KABOBS

- **2 cups (12-ounce package) NESTLÉ® TOLL HOUSE® Semi-Sweet Chocolate Morsels**
- **2 tablespoons vegetable shortening**
- **24 bite-size pieces pound cake**
- **24 bite-size pieces fresh fruit or berries (pineapple, banana, melon, strawberries)**

STRAWBERRY SAUCE

- **1 package (10 ounces) frozen strawberries in syrup, thawed**
- **3 tablespoons or more granulated sugar**

FOR KABOBS:

LINE baking sheet with waxed paper.

MICROWAVE morsels and vegetable shortening in a medium, uncovered, microwave-safe bowl on HIGH (100%) power for 1 minute; STIR. Morsels may retain some of their original shape. If necessary, microwave at additional 10- to 15-second intervals, stirring until smooth. Dip cake pieces into chocolate mixture; shake off excess. Place on prepared baking sheet; drizzle tops with additional chocolate. Refrigerate until set. On skewers, alternately thread chocolate coated pieces of cake with pieces of fruit; refrigerate. Serve with Strawberry Sauce.

FOR STRAWBERRY SAUCE:

PURÉE strawberries and sugar in blender until smooth.

Marshmallow Pops

20 **lollipop sticks (found at cake decorating or craft stores)**

20 **large marshmallows**

1 **cup (6 ounces) NESTLÉ® TOLL HOUSE® Premier White Morsels**

1 **cup (6 ounces) NESTLÉ® TOLL HOUSE® Milk Chocolate Morsels**

Decorating icing

Assorted NESTLÉ® Candies and Chocolate*

*NESTLÉ® RAISINETS®, NESTLÉ® SNO-CAPS®, WONKA® NERDS®, WONKA® TART N TINYS® and/or SweeTARTS® Gummy Bugs

LINE baking sheet with wax paper.

PUSH each lollipop stick halfway through a large marshmallow; set aside.

MELT white morsels according to package directions. Immediately dip *10* marshmallow lollipops lightly in the melted morsels for a thin coating. Set stick-side-up on prepared baking sheet.

MELT milk chocolate morsels according to package directions. Repeat dipping process as above with *remaining* marshmallows.

REFRIGERATE marshmallow lollipops for 10 minutes or until hardened. Use decorating icing as glue to decorate with assorted candies.

TOLL HOUSE® Chocolate Chip Cookie Milkshake

Makes 3 servings

1 **pint (2 cups) vanilla ice cream**

2 **cups (about 8 cookies) NESTLÉ® TOLL HOUSE® Refrigerated Chocolate Chip Cookie Dough, freshly baked and crumbled**

1 **cup milk** *or* **⅔ cup (5 fluid-ounce can) NESTLÉ® CARNATION® Evaporated Milk, chilled**

PLACE ice cream, cookies and 1 cup milk *or* ⅔ cup (5 fluid-ounce can) NESTLÉ® CARNATION® Evaporated Milk in blender; cover. Blend until smooth. If a smoother shake is desired, add some additional milk.

Chocolatey Chocolate Chip Cookie Cups

Makes 2 dozen cookie cups

1 **package (16.5 ounces) NESTLÉ® TOLL HOUSE® Refrigerated Chocolate Chip Cookie Bar Dough**

1 **cup (6 ounces) NESTLÉ® TOLL HOUSE® Peanut Butter & Milk Chocolate Morsels**

PREHEAT oven to 350° F. Grease or paper-line 24 mini muffin cups.

PLACE squares of dough into prepared muffin cups; press down lightly in center to make a well.

BAKE for 9 to 11 minutes or until edges are set. Cool in pans on wire racks for 5 minutes; remove to wire racks to cool completely.

MICROWAVE morsels in small, *heavy-duty* plastic bag on MEDIUM-HIGH (70%) power for 30 seconds; knead until smooth. Microwave at additional 10- to 15-second intervals, kneading until smooth. Cut tiny corner from bag; squeeze chocolate into each cup.

For Extra Chocolatey Chocolate Chip Cookie Cups:
SUBSTITUTE 1 cup (6 ounces) NESTLÉ® TOLL HOUSE® Semi-Sweet Chocolate Morsels for Peanut Butter & Milk Chocolate Morsels.

TOLL HOUSE® Chocolate Chip Cookie Milkshake

Dark Chocolate Orange Fondue

Makes 10 servings
(2 tablespoons per serving)

⅔ **cup heavy whipping cream**

2 **bars (8 ounces) NESTLÉ® TOLL HOUSE® Dark Chocolate Baking Bar, finely chopped**

1 **tablespoon orange liqueur (optional)**

1 **teaspoon grated orange peel**

Marshmallows, fresh fruit (washed and patted dry), cake cubes and/or pretzels

HEAT cream in small, *heavy-duty* saucepan over MEDIUM-HIGH heat; bring just to a boil. Remove from heat. Add chocolate; stir until smooth. Add liqueur and orange peel; mix well.

TRANSFER fondue to fondue pot; place over low heat. To serve, dip marshmallows, fruit, cake and/or pretzels into melted chocolate. Stir often while on heat. Makes 1¼ cups.

Marshmallow Sandwich Cookies

Makes 8 sandwich cookies

1 package (16.5 ounces) NESTLÉ® TOLL HOUSE® Refrigerated Chocolate Chip Cookie Dough*

8 large marshmallows

Or substitute dough from one batch Original NESTLÉ® TOLL HOUSE® Chocolate Chip Cookies (NESTLÉ® TOLL HOUSE® Semi-Sweet Chocolate Morsels 6-ounce package recipe).

PREPARE refrigerated cookie dough according to package directions. (If using dough from one batch Original cookie dough, make 16 cookies, baked 9 to 11 minutes.) Cool on baking sheets on wire racks for 1 minute; remove to wire racks to cool completely.

PLACE marshmallow on bottom side of one cookie. Microwave on MEDIUM (50%) power for 10 to 20 seconds or until marshmallow expands. Top with second cookie. Cool for 1 to 2 minutes. Repeat with remaining cookies and marshmallows.

Cookies & Cream Fudge

3 **cups granulated sugar**

¾ **cup (1½ sticks) butter or margarine**

⅔ **cup (5 fluid-ounce can) NESTLÉ® CARNATION® Evaporated Milk**

2 **cups (12-ounce package) NESTLÉ® TOLL HOUSE® Premier White Morsels**

1 **jar (7 ounces) marshmallow crème**

½ **cup finely crushed cream-filled chocolate sandwich cookies**

1 **teaspoon vanilla extract (optional)**

1 **cup crumbled cream-filled chocolate sandwich cookies**

LINE 9-inch-square baking pan with foil.

COMBINE sugar, butter and evaporated milk in medium, *heavy-duty* saucepan. Bring to a *full rolling boil*, stirring constantly. Boil, stirring constantly, for 3 minutes. Remove from heat.

STIR in morsels, marshmallow crème, finely crushed cookies and vanilla extract. Pour into prepared pan. Sprinkle crumbled cookies on top. Gently swirl cookies into fudge using a knife without touching bottom of pan. Refrigerate for 1 hour or until firm. Lift from pan; remove foil. Cut into 48 pieces. Store in airtight container in refrigerator.

NESTLÉ® TOLL HOUSE® Cookie S'mores

Makes 2 dozen S'mores

48 **graham cracker squares,**
  divided

1 **package (16.5 ounces)**
  NESTLÉ® TOLL HOUSE®
  Refrigerated Chocolate
  Chip Cookie Bar Dough

12 **large marshmallows, cut in**
  half

PREHEAT oven to 350° F. Line baking sheet with foil. Arrange *24* graham cracker squares on prepared baking sheet; set aside.

BAKE cookie dough on another baking sheet according to package instructions. Cool for 2 minutes on baking sheet. Remove cookies from baking sheet and place one warm cookie on each graham cracker square on foil. Top each cookie with one marshmallow half.

BAKE for 1 to 2 minutes or until marshmallows are soft. Immediately top s'mores with *remaining* graham cracker squares.

Easy Double Chocolate Chip Brownies

Makes 2 dozen brownies

2 cups (12-ounce package) NESTLÉ® TOLL HOUSE® Semi-Sweet Chocolate Morsels, *divided*

½ cup (1 stick) butter or margarine, cut into pieces

3 large eggs

1¼ cups all-purpose flour

1 cup granulated sugar

1 teaspoon vanilla extract

¼ teaspoon baking soda

½ cup chopped nuts

PREHEAT oven to 350° F. Grease 13×9-inch baking pan.

MELT *1 cup* morsels and butter in large, *heavy-duty* saucepan over low heat; stir until smooth. Remove from heat. Stir in eggs. Stir in flour, sugar, vanilla extract and baking soda. Stir in *remaining* morsels and nuts. Spread into prepared baking pan.

BAKE for 18 to 22 minutes or until wooden pick inserted in center comes out slightly sticky. Cool completely in pan on wire rack. Cut into bars.

Chocolate Angel Food Cake

1 **package (14.5 to 16 ounces) angel food cake mix**

½ **cup NESTLÉ® TOLL HOUSE® Baking Cocoa**

Powdered sugar

Strawberries (optional)

PREHEAT oven according to cake mix package directions.

COMBINE cake mix and cocoa in large mixer bowl. Prepare and bake according to cake mix package directions. Sprinkle with powdered sugar; top with strawberries.

Mini Morsel Ice Cream Pie

1½ **cups graham cracker crumbs**

½ **cup (1 stick) butter, melted**

¼ **cup granulated sugar**

1 **cup (6 ounces) NESTLÉ® TOLL HOUSE® Semi-Sweet Chocolate Mini Morsels**

1 **quart vanilla ice cream, softened**

COMBINE graham cracker crumbs, butter and sugar in medium bowl; stir in morsels. Press 2½ *cups* crumb mixture evenly on bottom and side of 9-inch pie plate. Freeze for 15 minutes or until firm. Spread softened ice cream evenly in pie shell. Top with *remaining* crumb mixture; freeze for 2 hours or until firm.

Chocolate Velvet Pie

1 *prepared* 8-inch (6 ounces) chocolate crumb crust

1¾ cups (11.5-ounce package) NESTLÉ® TOLL HOUSE® Milk Chocolate Morsels

1 package (8 ounces) cream cheese, softened

1 teaspoon vanilla extract

1 cup heavy whipping cream, whipped

Sweetened whipped cream (optional)

2 ounces NESTLÉ® TOLL HOUSE® Semi-Sweet Chocolate Baking Bar, made into curls*

Chopped nuts (optional)

For chocolate curls, carefully draw a vegetable peeler across edge of a bar of NESTLÉ® TOLL HOUSE® Semi-Sweet Chocolate.

MICROWAVE morsels in medium, uncovered, microwave-safe bowl on MEDIUM-HIGH (70%) power for 1 minute; STIR. Morsels may retain some of their original shape. If necessary, microwave at additional 10- to 15-second intervals, stirring just until melted. Cool to room temperature.

BEAT melted chocolate, cream cheese and vanilla extract in large mixer bowl until light in color. Fold in whipped cream. Spoon into crust. Refrigerate at least 2 hours or until firm. Top with sweetened whipped cream, chocolate curls and nuts.

Cookie Jar Collection

Want to bring the hit to this year's cookie exchange?
Whether you're looking for classic or jumbo cookies
made with chocolate, nuts, or something a little spicy,
the Nestlé® cookie collection has it all.

Big Chocolate Chunk Nut Cookies

Makes 7 cookies

1 package (16.5 ounces)
   NESTLÉ® TOLL HOUSE®
   Refrigerated Chocolate
   Chunk Cookie Bar Dough

½ cup coarsely chopped
   almonds, macadamia nuts,
   pecans and/or walnuts

PREHEAT oven to 350° F.

CRUMBLE cookie dough into medium bowl. Add nuts; mix thoroughly. Drop by ¼-cup measure onto ungreased baking sheets.

BAKE for 14 to 16 minutes or until golden brown. Cool on baking sheets for 1 minute; remove to wire racks to cool completely.

Chunky Chocolate Chip Peanut Butter Cookies

Makes about 3 dozen cookies

1¼ cups all-purpose flour

½ teaspoon baking soda

½ teaspoon salt

½ teaspoon ground cinnamon

¾ cup (1½ sticks) butter or margarine, softened

½ cup granulated sugar

½ cup packed brown sugar

½ cup creamy peanut butter

1 large egg

1 teaspoon vanilla extract

2 cups (12-ounce package) NESTLÉ® TOLL HOUSE® Semi-Sweet Chocolate Morsels

½ cup coarsely chopped peanuts

PREHEAT oven to 375° F.

COMBINE flour, baking soda, salt and cinnamon in small bowl. Beat butter, granulated sugar, brown sugar and peanut butter in large mixer bowl until creamy. Beat in egg and vanilla extract. Gradually beat in flour mixture. Stir in morsels and peanuts.

DROP dough by rounded tablespoon onto ungreased baking sheets. Press down slightly to flatten into 2-inch circles.

BAKE for 7 to 10 minutes or until edges are set but centers are still soft. Cool on baking sheets for 4 minutes; remove to wire racks to cool completely.

Chocolate Oatmeal Chippers

Makes about 4 dozen cookies

1¼ cups all-purpose flour

½ cup NESTLÉ® TOLL HOUSE® Baking Cocoa

1 teaspoon baking soda

¼ teaspoon salt

1 cup (2 sticks) butter or margarine, softened

1 cup packed brown sugar

½ cup granulated sugar

1 teaspoon vanilla extract

2 large eggs

1¾ cups (11.5-ounce package) NESTLÉ® TOLL HOUSE® Milk Chocolate Morsels

1¾ cups quick or old-fashioned oats

1 cup chopped nuts (optional)

PREHEAT oven to 375° F.

COMBINE flour, cocoa, baking soda and salt in medium bowl. Beat butter, brown sugar, granulated sugar and vanilla extract in large mixer bowl until creamy. Beat in eggs. Gradually beat in flour mixture. Stir in morsels, oats and nuts. Drop dough by rounded tablespoon onto ungreased baking sheets.

BAKE for 9 to 12 minutes or until edges are set but centers are still soft. Cool on baking sheets for 2 minutes; remove to wire racks to cool completely.

Bar Cookie Variation:

Preheat oven to 350° F. Grease 15×10-inch jelly-roll pan. Prepare dough as above. Spread into prepared pan. Bake for 25 to 30 minutes. Cool in pan on wire rack. Makes about 4 dozen bars.

Chocolate Caliente Cookies

1¾ cups (11.5-ounce package) **NESTLÉ® TOLL HOUSE® Semi-Sweet Chocolate Chunks**, *divided*

1½ cups all-purpose flour

1½ teaspoons ground cinnamon

1 teaspoon baking powder

¼ teaspoon salt

¹⁄₁₆ teaspoon (pinch) ground cayenne pepper

½ cup (1 stick) butter, softened

½ cup granulated sugar

½ cup packed light brown sugar

2 large eggs

1 teaspoon vanilla extract

MICROWAVE *1 cup* chunks in medium, uncovered, microwave-safe bowl on HIGH (100%) power for 1 minute; STIR. Chunks may retain some of their original shape. If necessary, microwave at additional 10- to 15-second intervals, stirring just until chunks are melted.

COMBINE flour, cinnamon, baking powder, salt and cayenne pepper in small bowl. Beat butter, granulated sugar and brown sugar in large mixer bowl until creamy. Add eggs and vanilla extract; beat well. Add melted chocolate; stir until blended. Gradually stir in flour mixture. Refrigerate for 2 hours.

PREHEAT oven to 350° F. Line baking sheets with foil.

SHAPE dough into 1½-inch balls. Place 3 inches apart on baking sheets.

BAKE for 12 minutes or until cookies are puffed and centers are set but still soft. Immediately place *remaining* chunks, about 5 to 6 chunks per cookie, onto tops of cookies. Cool on baking sheets for 2 minutes; remove to wire racks. Allow chunks to soften and spread melted chocolate evenly over tops of cookies.

Jumbo Dark Chocolate Cookies

Makes 1 dozen cookies

1⅔ cups (10-ounce package) **NESTLÉ® TOLL HOUSE® Dark Chocolate Morsels,** *divided*

1 cup all-purpose flour

¼ cup **NESTLÉ® TOLL HOUSE® Baking Cocoa**

1 teaspoon baking soda

½ teaspoon salt

½ cup (1 stick) butter, softened

½ cup packed light brown sugar

¼ cup granulated sugar

1 large egg

1 teaspoon vanilla extract

PREHEAT oven to 325° F. Line baking sheets with parchment paper or lightly grease.

MELT *⅔ cup* morsels in microwave-safe bowl on MEDIUM-HIGH (70%) power for 30 seconds; STIR. Morsels may retain some of their original shape. If necessary, microwave at additional 10- to 15-second intervals, stirring just until morsels are melted. Set aside.

SIFT flour, cocoa, baking soda and salt into medium bowl. Beat butter, brown sugar and granulated sugar in large mixer bowl until creamy. Add melted chocolate and mix well. Add egg and vanilla extract, mixing until well blended, about 1 minute. Add flour mixture, mixing just until blended. Stir in *remaining 1 cup* morsels. Drop dough by level ¼-cup measure 3 inches apart onto prepared baking sheets.

BAKE for 16 to 18 minutes or until wooden pick inserted in center comes out with moist crumbs and the tops have a cracked appearance. Cool on baking sheets for 5 minutes. Remove to wire racks to cool completely.

Sweet & Salty NESTLÉ® TOLL HOUSE® Cookies

Makes 5 dozen cookies

2¼ cups all-purpose flour

1 teaspoon baking soda

1 teaspoon salt (optional)

1 cup (2 sticks) butter, softened

¾ cup granulated sugar

¾ cup packed brown sugar

1 teaspoon vanilla extract

2 large eggs

2 cups (12-ounce package) NESTLÉ® TOLL HOUSE® Semi-Sweet Chocolate Morsels

2 cups coarsely broken rippled potato chips

1 cup small pretzel twists, broken into ½-inch pieces

½ cup unsalted peanuts (optional)

PREHEAT oven to 375° F.

COMBINE flour, baking soda and salt in small bowl. Beat butter, granulated sugar, brown sugar and vanilla extract in large mixer bowl until creamy. Add eggs, one at a time, beating well after each addition. Gradually beat in flour mixture. Stir in morsels, potato chips, pretzel pieces and peanuts. Drop by rounded tablespoon onto ungreased baking sheets.

BAKE for 9 to 11 minutes or until golden brown. Cool on baking sheets for 2 minutes; remove to wire racks to cool completely.

Dark Chocolate Chip & Trail Mix Cookies

Makes 54 cookies

2 cups all-purpose flour

1 teaspoon baking soda

1 teaspoon salt

1 cup (2 sticks) butter, softened

⅔ cup granulated sugar

⅔ cup packed brown sugar

1 teaspoon vanilla extract

2 large eggs

1⅔ cups (10-ounce package) NESTLÉ® TOLL HOUSE® Dark Chocolate Morsels

2 cups lowfat granola cereal

2 cups coarsely chopped dried apricots, cranberries, blueberries and/or cherries

PREHEAT oven to 375° F.

COMBINE flour, baking soda and salt in small bowl. Beat butter, granulated sugar, brown sugar and vanilla extract in large mixer bowl until creamy. Add eggs, one at a time, beating well after each addition. Gradually beat in flour mixture. Stir in morsels, granola and dried fruit. Drop by rounded tablespoon onto ungreased baking sheets.

BAKE for 10 to 12 minutes or until golden brown. Cool on baking sheets for 2 minutes; remove to wire racks to cool completely.

TIP:

Substitute your favorite dried fruits.

Chocolate Mint Brownie Cookies

Makes 3 dozen cookies

1½ cups (9 ounces) NESTLÉ® TOLL HOUSE® Semi-Sweet Chocolate Morsels, *divided*

1¾ cups all-purpose flour

½ teaspoon baking soda

¼ teaspoon salt

½ cup (1 stick) butter or margarine, softened

½ cup granulated sugar

¼ cup packed brown sugar

½ teaspoon peppermint extract

½ teaspoon vanilla extract

2 large eggs

¾ cup chopped nuts

PREHEAT oven to 350° F.

MELT ¾ *cup* morsels in small, *heavy-duty* saucepan over *lowest possible* heat. When morsels begin to melt, remove from heat; stir. Return to heat for a few seconds at a time, stirring until smooth. Cool to room temperature.

COMBINE flour, baking soda and salt in small bowl. Beat butter, granulated sugar, brown sugar, peppermint extract and vanilla extract in large mixer bowl until creamy. Add eggs, one at a time, beating well after each addition. Beat in melted chocolate. Gradually beat in flour mixture. Stir in *remaining ¾ cup* morsels and nuts. Drop dough by rounded tablespoon onto ungreased baking sheets.

BAKE for 8 to 12 minutes or until sides are set but centers are still soft. Let stand for 2 minutes; remove to wire racks to cool completely.

Molasses Spice Cookies

1¾ **cups all-purpose flour**

1 **teaspoon baking soda**

1 **teaspoon ground ginger**

1 **teaspoon ground cinnamon**

¼ **teaspoon ground cloves**

¼ **teaspoon salt**

1 **cup granulated sugar**

¾ **cup (1½ sticks) butter or margarine, softened**

1 **large egg**

¼ **cup unsulphured molasses**

2 **cups (12-ounce package) NESTLÉ® TOLL HOUSE® Premier White Morsels**

1 **cup finely chopped walnuts**

COMBINE flour, baking soda, ginger, cinnamon, cloves and salt in small bowl. Beat sugar and butter in large mixer bowl until creamy. Beat in egg and molasses. Gradually beat in flour mixture. Stir in morsels. Refrigerate for 20 minutes or until slightly firm.

PREHEAT oven to 375° F.

ROLL dough into 1-inch balls; roll in walnuts. Place on ungreased baking sheets.

BAKE for 9 to 11 minutes or until golden brown. Cool on baking sheets for 2 minutes; remove to wire racks to cool completely.

Milk Chocolate Florentine Cookies

Makes about 3½ dozen sandwich cookies

⅔ **cup butter**

2 **cups quick oats**

1 **cup granulated sugar**

⅔ **cup all-purpose flour**

¼ **cup light or dark corn syrup**

¼ **cup milk**

1 **teaspoon vanilla extract**

¼ **teaspoon salt**

1¾ **cups (11.5-ounce package) NESTLÉ® TOLL HOUSE® Milk Chocolate Morsels**

PREHEAT oven to 375° F. Line baking sheets with foil.

MELT butter in medium saucepan; remove from heat. Stir in oats, sugar, flour, corn syrup, milk, vanilla extract and salt; mix well. Drop by level teaspoon, about 3 inches apart, onto prepared baking sheets. Spread thinly with rubber spatula.

BAKE for 6 to 8 minutes or until golden brown. Cool completely on baking sheets on wire racks. Peel foil from cookies.

MICROWAVE morsels in medium, uncovered, microwave-safe bowl on MEDIUM-HIGH (70%) power for 1 minute; STIR. Morsels may retain some of their original shape. If necessary, microwave at additional 10- to 15-second intervals, stirring just until morsels are melted. Spread thin layer of melted chocolate onto flat side of *half* the cookies. Top with *remaining* cookies to make sandwiches.

Jumbo 3-Chip Cookies

Makes about 2 dozen cookies

4 **cups all-purpose flour**

1 **teaspoon baking powder**

1 **teaspoon baking soda**

1½ **cups (3 sticks) butter, softened**

1¼ **cups granulated sugar**

1¼ **cups packed brown sugar**

2 **large eggs**

1 **tablespoon vanilla extract**

1 **cup (6 ounces) NESTLÉ® TOLL HOUSE® Milk Chocolate Morsels**

1 **cup (6 ounces) NESTLÉ® TOLL HOUSE® Semi-Sweet Chocolate Morsels**

½ **cup NESTLÉ® TOLL HOUSE® Premier White Morsels**

1 **cup chopped nuts**

PREHEAT oven to 375° F.

COMBINE flour, baking powder and baking soda in medium bowl. Beat butter, granulated sugar and brown sugar in large mixer bowl until creamy. Beat in eggs and vanilla extract. Gradually beat in flour mixture. Stir in morsels and nuts. Drop dough by level ¼-cup measure 2 inches apart onto ungreased baking sheets.

BAKE for 12 to 14 minutes or until light golden brown. Cool on baking sheets for 2 minutes; remove to wire racks to cool completely.

Zucchini-Oat Dark Chocolate Chip Cookies

Makes 4 dozen cookies

1½ **cups all-purpose flour**

1 **teaspoon ground cinnamon**

½ **teaspoon baking soda**

½ **cup (1 stick) butter, softened**

¾ **cup granulated sugar**

1 **large egg**

¾ **teaspoon vanilla extract**

1½ **cups shredded zucchini (1 medium)**

1 **cup quick oats**

1 **cup chopped nuts**

1⅔ **cups (10-ounce package) NESTLÉ® TOLL HOUSE® Dark Chocolate Morsels**

PREHEAT oven to 350° F. Lightly grease baking sheets.

COMBINE flour, cinnamon and baking soda in small bowl. Beat butter, sugar in large mixer bowl until well combined. Add egg and vanilla extract, beat well. Add zucchini; gradually beat in flour mixture. Stir in oats, nuts and morsels. Drop by rounded teaspoon 2 inches apart onto prepared baking sheets.

BAKE for 9 to 11 minutes or until light golden brown around edges. Cool on baking sheets for 2 minutes; remove to wire rack to cool completely. Store in tightly covered container at room temperature.

Frosted Double Chocolate Cookies

Makes 15 cookies

2 **cups (12-ounce package) NESTLÉ® TOLL HOUSE® Semi-Sweet Chocolate Morsels,** *divided*

1¼ **cups all-purpose flour**

¾ **teaspoon baking soda**

½ **teaspoon salt**

½ **cup (1 stick) butter or margarine, softened**

½ **cup packed brown sugar**

¼ **cup granulated sugar**

1 **teaspoon vanilla extract**

1 **large egg**

½ **cup chopped nuts (optional)**

CHOCOLATE FROSTING

2 **tablespoons butter or margarine**

1¼ **cups sifted powdered sugar**

2 **tablespoons milk**

PREHEAT oven to 375° F.

MICROWAVE *¾ cup* morsels in small, uncovered, microwave-safe bowl on HIGH (100%) power for 1 minute; STIR. Morsels may retain some of their original shape. If necessary, microwave at additional 10- to 15-second intervals, stirring just until morsels are melted. Cool to room temperature. Combine flour, baking soda and salt in small bowl.

BEAT butter, brown sugar, granulated sugar and vanilla extract in large mixer bowl until creamy. Beat in melted chocolate and egg. Gradually beat in flour mixture. Stir in *¾ cup* morsels and nuts. Drop by rounded tablespoon onto ungreased baking sheets.

BAKE for 8 to 9 minutes or until edges are set but centers are still slightly soft. Cool on baking sheets for 3 minutes; remove to wire racks to cool completely. Thinly frost centers of cookies with Chocolate Frosting.

FOR CHOCOLATE FROSTING:

MICROWAVE *remaining ½ cup* morsels and butter in medium, uncovered, microwave-safe bowl on HIGH (100%) power for 30 seconds; STIR. Microwave at additional 10- to 15-second intervals, stirring until smooth. Add powdered sugar and milk; stir until smooth.

Chocolate-Cherry Thumbprints

Makes about 4 dozen cookies

2 cups (12-ounce package) **NESTLÉ® TOLL HOUSE® Semi-Sweet Chocolate Morsels,** *divided*

1¾ cups quick or old-fashioned oats

1½ cups all-purpose flour

¼ cup **NESTLÉ® TOLL HOUSE® Baking Cocoa**

1 teaspoon baking powder

¼ teaspoon salt (optional)

¾ cup granulated sugar

⅔ cup butter or margarine, softened

2 large eggs

1 teaspoon vanilla extract

2 cups (two 10-ounce jars) maraschino cherries, drained and patted dry

MICROWAVE *1 cup* morsels in small, uncovered, microwave-safe bowl on HIGH (100%) power for 1 minute; STIR. Morsels may retain some of their original shape. If necessary, microwave at additional 10- to 15-second intervals, stirring just until morsels are melted. Combine oats, flour, cocoa, baking powder and salt in medium bowl.

BEAT sugar, butter, eggs and vanilla extract in large mixer bowl until smooth. Beat in melted chocolate. Stir in oat mixture. Cover; refrigerate dough for 1 hour.

PREHEAT oven to 350° F.

SHAPE dough into 1-inch balls; press thumb into tops to make deep depression. Place 2 inches apart on ungreased baking sheets. Place maraschino cherry into each depression.

BAKE for 10 to 12 minutes or until set. Cool on baking sheets for 2 minutes; remove to wire racks to cool completely. Melt *remaining* morsels; drizzle over cookies.

Blueberry-White Morsels Biscotti

Makes 2 dozen biscotti

1 package (18.25 to 18.9 ounces) blueberry muffin mix with can of blueberries

¾ cup all-purpose flour

½ cup (1 stick) butter, melted and cooled slightly

2 large eggs, slightly beaten

2 cups (12-ounce package) NESTLÉ® TOLL HOUSE® Premier White Morsels, *divided*

PREHEAT oven to 350° F. Grease two baking sheets. Drain blueberries; set aside.

COMBINE muffin mix, flour, butter and eggs just until combined in large bowl. Fold in *1½ cups* morsels and drained blueberries with floured hands. Shape *half* of dough into a 12-inch-long roll (dough may be sticky). Place on a prepared baking sheet; flatten slightly until about 2 inches wide. Repeat with *remaining* dough.

BAKE for about 25 minutes or until wooden pick inserted near the centers comes out clean. Cool on baking sheets on wire racks for 1 hour.

CUT each roll diagonally into ¾-inch slices with serrated knife. Place slices, cut side down, on ungreased baking sheets.

BAKE for 10 minutes. Turn slices over and bake additional 6 to 8 minutes or until light brown (do not overbake). Transfer to wire racks and let cool.

PLACE *remaining* morsels in small, *heavy-duty* plastic bag. Microwave on HIGH (100%) power for 20 seconds; knead bag to mix. Microwave at additional 10-second intervals, kneading until smooth. Cut a small hole in corner of bag; squeeze to drizzle biscotti. Let stand until drizzle is set. Store in an airtight container at room temperature up to 24 hours or freeze up to 3 months for longer storage.

Milk Chocolate Oatmeal Cookies

Makes about 3 dozen cookies

1¼ cups all-purpose flour

½ teaspoon baking powder

½ teaspoon baking soda

½ teaspoon ground cinnamon

¼ teaspoon salt

¾ cup (1½ sticks) butter or margarine, softened

¾ cup packed brown sugar

⅓ cup granulated sugar

1½ teaspoons vanilla extract

1 large egg

2 tablespoons milk

1¾ cups (11.5-ounce package) NESTLÉ® TOLL HOUSE® Milk Chocolate Morsels

1 cup quick or old-fashioned oats

½ cup raisins (optional)

PREHEAT oven to 375° F.

COMBINE flour, baking powder, baking soda, cinnamon and salt in small bowl. Beat butter, brown sugar, granulated sugar and vanilla extract in large mixer bowl until creamy. Beat in egg. Gradually beat in flour mixture and milk. Stir in morsels, oats and raisins. Drop by rounded tablespoon onto ungreased baking sheets.

BAKE for 10 to 14 minutes or until edges are crisp but centers are still soft. Cool on baking sheets for 2 minutes; remove to wire racks to cool completely.

White Chip Chocolate Cookies

Makes 5 dozen cookies

2¼ cups all-purpose flour

⅔ cup NESTLÉ® TOLL HOUSE®
   Baking Cocoa

1 teaspoon baking soda

¼ teaspoon salt

1 cup (2 sticks) butter or
   margarine, softened

¾ cup granulated sugar

⅔ cup packed brown sugar

1 teaspoon vanilla extract

2 large eggs

2 cups (12-ounce package)
   NESTLÉ® TOLL HOUSE®
   Premier White Morsels

PREHEAT oven to 350° F.

COMBINE flour, cocoa, baking soda and salt in small bowl. Beat butter, granulated sugar, brown sugar and vanilla extract in large mixer bowl until creamy. Add eggs, one at a time, beating well after each addition. Gradually beat in flour mixture. Stir in morsels. Drop by well-rounded teaspoon onto ungreased baking sheets.

BAKE for 9 to 11 minutes or until centers are set. Cool on baking sheets for 2 minutes; remove to wire racks to cool completely.

Salty Peanut Butter S'more

1 package (16.5 ounces) NESTLÉ® TOLL HOUSE® Ultimates™ Peanut Butter Lovers Cookies

12 large marshmallows

6 ounces NESTLÉ® TOLL HOUSE® Semi-Sweet Chocolate Baking Bar, broken in squares

⅓ cup caramel ice cream topping

¼ cup chopped peanuts

PREHEAT oven to 325° F. Cut each square of cookie dough in half (total of 24 half pieces are needed for the recipe.) Place 2 inches apart on ungreased baking sheets.

BAKE for 10 to 12 minutes or until golden brown. Cool on baking sheets for 2 minutes; remove to wire racks to cool.

TO ASSEMBLE:

SPREAD small amount of ice cream topping on flat side of 12 cookies; place on wire rack.

PLACE *remaining* 12 baked cookies flat side up on cooled baking sheet. Place 1 marshmallow on top of each cookie.

BAKE for 1 to 2 minutes or until marshmallows are soft. Immediately top each marshmallow with a square of chocolate and a reserved cookie. Gently squeeze cookies together to make a sandwich. Roll sides of sandwiches in peanuts. Cookies are best when eaten slightly warm!

Football Cookies

1 package (16.5 ounces) NESTLÉ® TOLL HOUSE® Refrigerated Chocolate Chip Cookie Bar Dough,* softened at room temperature for 30 minutes

⅓ cup NESTLÉ® TOLL HOUSE® Baking Cocoa, plus additional for rolling

3-inch football cutter

Decorator icings (various colors)

Red or black thin licorice rope

*2 cups NESTLÉ® TOLL HOUSE® Refrigerated Chocolate Chip Tub Dough can be substituted for the bar dough.

PREHEAT oven to 325° F. Grease two baking sheets.

COMBINE softened cookie dough and cocoa in large mixer bowl. This can be done with a mixer or with clean hands.

ROLL dough to ¼-inch thickness between sheets of wax paper, using additional cocoa to prevent sticking. Cut out footballs with cookie cutter. Place 1 inch apart on prepared baking sheets. Repeat with trimmings.

BAKE for 12 to 13 minutes or until edges are set. (If using dark baking sheets, check at 12 minutes.) Cool for 2 minutes; remove to wire racks to cool completely.

DECORATE cookies with icings as desired. Cut licorice into small pieces to form laces. Let stand for 15 minutes to set icing. Store cookies in between wax paper layers in covered container.

Fun Finger Foods

Celebrate any occasion with these scrumptious finger foods.
Discover grown-up goodies like Dark Chocolate Truffles
or Macaroon Butterscotch Tartlets.
For the kid-friendly gatherings, try Peanut Butter Fudge,
Milk Chocolate Popcorn, and so much more.

Peanut Butter Fudge

Makes 24 servings (2 pieces per serving)

- 1½ cups granulated sugar
- ⅔ cup (5 fluid-ounce can) NESTLÉ® CARNATION® Evaporated Milk
- 2 tablespoons butter or margarine
- ¼ teaspoon salt
- 2 cups miniature marshmallows
- 1½ cups (9 ounces) NESTLÉ® TOLL HOUSE® Semi-Sweet Chocolate Morsels
- 1 cup chunky or regular peanut butter
- 1 teaspoon vanilla extract
- ½ cup chopped peanuts (optional)

COMBINE sugar, evaporated milk, butter and salt in a medium, *heavy-duty* saucepan. Bring to a *full rolling boil* over medium heat, stirring constantly. Boil, stirring constantly, for 4 to 5 minutes. Remove from heat.

STIR in marshmallows, morsels, peanut butter and vanilla extract. Stir vigorously for 1 minute or until marshmallows are melted. Pour into foil-lined 8-inch-square baking pan; cool for 1 minute. Top with peanuts, pressing in slightly. Refrigerate for 2 hours or until firm. Lift from pan; remove foil. Cut into 48 pieces.

Double Chocolate Chip Mini Cheesecakes

Makes 24 servings

1½ cups NESTLÉ® TOLL HOUSE® Refrigerated Chocolate Chip Cookie Tub Dough or 1 package (16.5 ounces) NESTLÉ® TOLL HOUSE® Refrigerated Chocolate Chip Cookie Bar Dough

2 packages (8 ounces *each*) cream cheese, at room temperature

¾ cup granulated sugar

2 tablespoons all-purpose flour

2 large eggs

1 teaspoon vanilla extract

¾ cup NESTLÉ® TOLL HOUSE® Semi-Sweet Chocolate Mini Morsels, *divided*

PREHEAT oven to 325° F. Paper-line 24 muffin cups. Place 1 level tablespoon of cookie dough (1 square if using bar dough) into each muffin cup.

BAKE for 10 minutes or until cookie has spread to edge of cup.

BEAT cream cheese, sugar and flour in large mixer bowl until creamy. Add eggs and vanilla extract; mix well. Stir ½ cup morsels into batter. Spoon 2 heaping measuring tablespoons of batter over each cookie in cup.

BAKE for additional 13 to 15 minutes or until just set but not browned. Remove from oven to wire rack. Cool completely in pans on wire rack. Refrigerate for 1 hour.

MELT *remaining ¼ cup* mini morsels in small, heavy-duty plastic bag on HIGH (100%) power for 30 seconds; knead. Microwave at additional 10- to 15-second intervals, kneading until smooth. Cut tiny corner from bag; squeeze to drizzle lightly over each cheesecake just before serving.

Milk Chocolate Popcorn

Makes 14 servings

12 cups popped corn

1 can (12 ounces) salted peanuts

1¾ cups (11.5-ounce package) NESTLÉ® TOLL HOUSE® Milk Chocolate Morsels

1 cup light corn syrup

¼ cup (½ stick) butter or margarine

PREHEAT oven to 300° F. Grease large roasting pan. Line serving plate with wax paper.

COMBINE popcorn and nuts in prepared roasting pan. Combine morsels, corn syrup and butter in medium, *heavy-duty* saucepan. Cook over medium heat, stirring constantly, until mixture boils. Pour over popcorn; toss well to coat.

BAKE, stirring frequently, for 30 to 40 minutes. Cool slightly in pan; remove to prepared serving plate. Store in airtight container for up to two weeks.

White Fudge with Crystallized Ginger & Cranberries

Makes 24 servings (2 pieces per serving)

1½ cups granulated sugar

1 teaspoon ground ginger

⅔ cup (5 fluid-ounce can) NESTLÉ® CARNATION® Evaporated Milk

2 tablespoons butter

2 cups miniature marshmallows

2 cups (12-ounce package) NESTLÉ® TOLL HOUSE® Premier White Morsels

1¼ cups (6-ounce package) sweetened dried cranberries, coarsely chopped

1 jar (2.5 ounces) or ½ cup crystallized ginger*

*Crystallized ginger can be found in the spice aisle of the grocery store.

LINE 8- or 9-inch-square baking pan with foil.

COMBINE sugar and ground ginger in medium, *heavy-duty* saucepan. Add evaporated milk and butter. Bring to a *full rolling boil* over medium heat, stirring constantly. Boil, stirring constantly, for 4 to 5 minutes (to 234° F). Remove from heat.

STIR in marshmallows, morsels, cranberries and crystallized ginger. Stir vigorously for 1 minute or until marshmallows are melted. Pour into prepared pan; refrigerate until firm, about 1½ hours. Lift from pan; remove foil. Cut into 48 pieces.

Milk Chocolate Popcorn

Mini Lemon Lime Tartlets

Makes 2 dozen tartlets

1 package (16.5 ounces) NESTLÉ® TOLL HOUSE® Refrigerated Sugar Cookie Bar Dough

1 can (14 ounces) NESTLÉ® CARNATION® Sweetened Condensed Milk

1 package (8 ounces) ⅓ less fat cream cheese (Neufchâtel) or regular cream cheese, at room temperature

2 cups thawed fat-free, reduced-fat or regular frozen whipped topping

¼ cup lemon juice

2 teaspoons grated lemon peel

¼ cup lime juice

2 teaspoons grated lime peel

Additional lemon and lime quarter slices, peel curls or grated peel (optional)

PREHEAT oven to 325° F. Paper-line 24 muffin cups.

CUT dough along pre-scored lines; place one piece of cookie dough in each muffin cup.

BAKE for 13 to 15 minutes or until golden brown. Cookies will be puffy. Cool completely in pan on wire rack.

BEAT sweetened condensed milk and cream cheese in large mixer bowl until smooth. Gently fold in whipped topping. Divide mixture into two medium bowls. Stir lemon juice and lemon peel into one bowl and lime juice and lime peel into other bowl.

POUR about 3 tablespoons lemon cream cheese mixture, followed by the lime cream cheese mixture, over 24 cookie cups. Refrigerate for 2 hours or overnight. Decorate with lemon and lime quarter slices, curls or peel, if desired.

Tips:

● Using low and reduced fat cream cheese and whipped topping helps to make these treats lower in fat.

● Love lemon but not crazy about lime? Simply double the lemon juice and grated lemon peel in the recipe and leave out the lime, and make 24 lemon tartlets. Tartlets may be frozen in an airtight container for up to 2 weeks. Allow to thaw at room temperature for 30 minutes before serving.

Chocolate-Dipped Fruit Kabobs

Makes 6 kabobs

1 cup (6 ounces) NESTLÉ® TOLL HOUSE® Semi-Sweet Chocolate Morsels

18 pieces bite-size fresh fruit, (strawberries, apple, banana, kiwifruit)

6 4-inch wooden skewers

LINE baking sheet with wax paper.

MICROWAVE morsels in small, uncovered, microwave-safe bowl on HIGH (100%) power for 1 minute; STIR. Morsels may retain some of their original shape. If necessary, microwave at additional 10- to 15-second intervals, stirring just until morsels are melted.

DIP fruit about halfway into chocolate; shake off excess. Or, place melted chocolate in small, *heavy-duty* plastic bag. Cut tiny corner from bag; squeeze to drizzle over fruit. Place fruit on prepared baking sheet. Refrigerate for 5 to 10 minutes or until chocolate is set.

THREAD three pieces fruit on each skewer.

Peanut Butterscotch Pretzel Snacks

Makes 5 dozen pretzels

1⅔ cups (11-ounce package) NESTLÉ® TOLL HOUSE® Butterscotch Flavored Morsels

⅓ cup creamy peanut butter

60 3-inch pretzel twists

2 to 3 tablespoons sesame seeds, toasted

MICROWAVE morsels and peanut butter in medium, uncovered, microwave-safe bowl on MEDIUM-HIGH (70%) power for 1 minute; STIR. Morsels may retain some of their original shape. If necessary, microwave at additional 10- to 15-second intervals, stirring just until morsels are melted.

DIP about ¾ of one pretzel in butterscotch mixture; shake off excess. Place on wire rack; sprinkle lightly with sesame seeds. Repeat with remaining pretzels. (If mixture thickens, microwave on MEDIUM-HIGH (70%) power at 10- to 15-second intervals, stirring until smooth.)

REFRIGERATE for 20 minutes or until set. Store in airtight containers or resealable plastic bags.

NESTLÉ® TOLL HOUSE® Spicy Party Mix

Makes 40 servings
(⅓ cup per serving)

1½ **quarts water**

1 **pound pecan halves**

½ **cup granulated sugar**

2 **tablespoons plus 1½ teaspoons canola oil**

1 **vanilla bean (optional)**

1 **teaspoon fine sea salt**

½ **teaspoon chili powder**

½ **teaspoon curry powder**

½ **teaspoon ground coriander**

½ **teaspoon ground cumin**

½ **teaspoon garlic salt**

¼ **teaspoon ground allspice**

¼ **teaspoon ground cinnamon**

¼ **teaspoon ground nutmeg**

¼ **teaspoon cayenne pepper (optional)**

2 **cups pretzel nuggets**

1¾ **cups (11.5-ounce package) NESTLÉ® TOLL HOUSE® Semi-Sweet Chocolate Chunks**

1 **package (6 ounces) sweetened dried cranberries**

BRING water to a boil in large saucepan. Pour nuts into boiling water. Boil for 1 minute; strain. Pour nuts into large bowl. Add sugar and oil; stir to coat. Let stand for 10 minutes.

SPLIT vanilla bean in half lengthwise and with edge of knife, scrape inside of bean into a large bowl. Add spices to bowl; combine well and set aside.

PREHEAT oven to 325° F.

BAKE nuts, stirring often, for 30 to 35 minutes or until nuts are light brown and crisp. While still warm, carefully pour nuts into spice mixture and toss. Spread spiced nuts in a single layer on clean, large baking sheet with sides. Cool completely.

POUR cooled nuts into large bowl. Add pretzel nuggets, chunks and cranberries; mix well. Store in airtight container at room temperature for up to 2 weeks. Makes 10 cups.

Macaroon Butterscotch Tartlets

Makes 12 tartlets

FILLING

- ⅔ **cup (5 fluid-ounce can) NESTLÉ® CARNATION® Evaporated Milk**
- ¼ **cup water**
- 2 **tablespoons cornstarch**
- ⅛ **teaspoon salt**
- ⅔ **cup NESTLÉ® TOLL HOUSE® Butterscotch Flavored Morsels**
- 1 **tablespoon butter**
- 1 **teaspoon vanilla extract**

CRUSTS

- 1½ **cups all-purpose flour**
- 1 **cup *plus* 2 tablespoons sweetened flaked coconut, *divided***
- 2 **tablespoons granulated sugar**
- **Pinch salt**
- ½ **cup (1 stick) butter, cut into small pieces**
- 1 **to 2 tablespoons water, *divided***

FOR BUTTERSCOTCH FILLING

WHISK together evaporated milk, water, cornstarch and salt in small saucepan. Cook over medium heat, *stirring constantly*, until mixture begins to thicken. Remove from heat. Stir in morsels, butter and vanilla extract until smooth. For a smoother sauce, strain through metal strainer. Refrigerate for 1 hour.

FOR COCONUT CRUSTS

PREHEAT oven to 375° F. Grease 12 (2½-inch) muffin cups. Line small baking sheet with foil.

PLACE flour, *1 cup* coconut, sugar and salt in food processor fitted with metal blade. Process until finely chopped. Add butter and *1 tablespoon* water and pulse until fine crumbs are formed. Divide mixture evenly between muffin cups and press onto bottom and halfway up sides. Pierce bottom of each crust several times.

BAKE crusts for 15 minutes or until light brown around edges, repiercing bottoms of crusts after 8 minutes. While baking the crust, toast *remaining 2 tablespoons* coconut on prepared baking sheet in same oven for 8 minutes or until light golden brown. Cool coconut crusts in cups and toasted coconut completely on wire racks.

TO SERVE, remove crusts from pans to serving platter with tip of knife. Spoon a heaping measuring tablespoon of Butterscotch Filling into each crust. Top with toasted coconut.

Layered Chocolate Caramel Candy

Makes 108 pieces

CHOCOLATE LAYER

1¾ cups (11.5-ounce package) NESTLÉ® TOLL HOUSE® Milk Chocolate Morsels, *divided*

½ cup NESTLÉ® TOLL HOUSE® Butterscotch Flavored Morsels, *divided*

¾ cup creamy peanut butter, *divided*

MARSHMALLOW LAYER

¼ cup (½ stick) butter

1 cup granulated sugar

¼ cup NESTLÉ® CARNATION® Evaporated Milk

1 jar (7 ounces) marshmallow crème

1 teaspoon vanilla extract

1½ cups lightly salted peanuts, coarsely chopped

CARAMEL LAYER

1 package (14 ounces) vanilla caramels

¼ cup heavy whipping cream

LINE 13×9-inch baking pan with foil; grease foil with butter.

FOR CHOCOLATE LAYER

HEAT *1 cup* milk chocolate morsels, *1/4 cup* butterscotch morsels and *1/4 cup* peanut butter in small saucepan over low heat, stirring frequently, until melted. Spread chocolate mixture over bottom of prepared baking pan; cover. Refrigerate for 20 minutes or until set.

FOR MARSHMALLOW LAYER

MELT butter in *heavy-duty* saucepan over medium heat. Add sugar and evaporated milk; heat to a boil. Cook, stirring occasionally, until sugar is dissolved. Reduce heat until mixture comes *just* to a boil. Heat for 5 minutes (*do not stir*); remove from heat. Stir in marshmallow crème, *1/4 cup* peanut butter and vanilla extract. Stir in peanuts. Carefully spoon marshmallow layer over chocolate layer; cover. Refrigerate for 20 minutes or until set.

FOR CARAMEL LAYER

HEAT caramels and cream in medium saucepan over low heat, stirring frequently, until caramels are melted and mixture is smooth. Spread caramel mixture over marshmallow layer; cover. Refrigerate for 15 to 30 minutes or until set.

FOR TOPPING

HEAT *remaining* morsels and *remaining* peanut butter in small saucepan over low heat, stirring frequently, until mixture is smooth. Spread over caramel layer. Refrigerate for at least 2 hours or overnight.

USE foil to lift candy from baking pan; remove foil. Cut into 1-inch pieces. Store in airtight container in refrigerator for up to 1 week.

Cheesecake Cookie Cups

1 package (16.5 ounces) NESTLÉ® TOLL HOUSE® Refrigerated Chocolate Chip Cookie Bar Dough

2 packages (8 ounces *each*) cream cheese, at room temperature

1 can (14 ounces) NESTLÉ® CARNATION® Sweetened Condensed Milk

2 large eggs

2 teaspoons vanilla extract

1 can (21 ounces) cherry pie filling

PREHEAT oven to 325° F. Paper-line 24 muffin cups. Place one piece of cookie dough in each muffin cup.

BAKE for 10 to 12 minutes or until cookie has spread to edge of cup.

BEAT cream cheese, sweetened condensed milk, eggs and vanilla extract in medium bowl until smooth. Pour about 3 tablespoons cream cheese mixture over each cookie in cup.

BAKE for additional 15 to 18 minutes or until set. Cool completely in pan on wire rack. Top each with level tablespoon of pie filling. Refrigerate for 1 hour.

TOLL HOUSE® Party Mix

Makes 8 servings

2 cups toasted cereal squares

2 cups small pretzel twists

1 cup dry-roasted peanuts

1 cup (about 20) caramels, unwrapped and coarsely chopped

1⅔ to 2 cups (11- to 12-ounce package) NESTLÉ® TOLL HOUSE® Semi-Sweet Chocolate, Milk Chocolate, Butterscotch Flavored or Premier White Morsels

COAT 13×9-inch baking pan with nonstick cooking spray.

COMBINE cereal, pretzels, peanuts and caramels in large bowl.

MICROWAVE morsels in medium, uncovered, microwave-safe bowl on MEDIUM-HIGH (70%) power for 1 minute; STIR. Morsels may retain some of their original shape. If necessary, microwave at additional 10- to 15-second intervals, stirring just until morsels are melted. Pour over cereal mixture; stir to coat evenly.

SPREAD mixture in prepared baking pan; cool for 30 to 45 minutes or until firm. Break into bite-size pieces. Store in airtight container.

Dark Chocolate Truffles

Makes about 3 to 4 dozen truffles

⅔ cup heavy whipping cream

1⅔ cups (10-ounce package)
   NESTLÉ® TOLL HOUSE®
   Dark Chocolate Morsels

Finely chopped toasted nuts,
   toasted flaked coconut
   and/or NESTLÉ®
   TOLL HOUSE® Baking
   Cocoa for coating truffles

LINE baking sheet with parchment or wax paper.

HEAT cream to a gentle boil in medium, *heavy-duty* saucepan. Remove from heat. Add chocolate. Stir until mixture is smooth and chocolate is melted. Refrigerate for 15 to 20 minutes or until slightly thickened.

DROP chocolate mixture by rounded measuring teaspoon onto prepared baking sheet. Refrigerate for 20 minutes. Shape or roll into balls; coat with nuts, coconut or cocoa. Store in airtight container in refrigerator.

Petit Pain au Chocolate

1   **package (17.25 ounces) frozen puff pastry sheets, thawed**

1   **cup (6 ounces) NESTLÉ® TOLL HOUSE® Milk Chocolate Morsels, *divided***

1   **large egg, beaten**

2   **ounces NESTLÉ® TOLL HOUSE® Semi-Sweet Chocolate Baking Bar, broken into pieces**

2   **tablespoons butter or margarine**

1   **cup powdered sugar**

2   **tablespoons hot water**

PREHEAT oven to 350° F. Grease two baking sheets.

UNFOLD *1* pastry sheet on lightly floured surface. Roll out to make 10-inch square. Cut into 4 squares. Place *2 tablespoons* morsels in center of each square. Brush edges lightly with beaten egg and fold squares to form triangles. Press edges to seal. Place on prepared baking sheet about 2 inches apart. Repeat with *remaining* pastry sheet. Brush top of each pastry with beaten egg.

BAKE for 15 to 17 minutes or until puffed and golden. Cool on baking sheets for 2 minutes; remove to wire racks to cool completely.

MELT broken baking bar and butter in small, uncovered, microwave-safe bowl on HIGH (100%) power for 30 seconds; STIR. If pieces retain some of their original shape, microwave at additional 10- to 15-second intervals, stirring just until smooth. Stir in sugar. Add water, stirring until icing is smooth, adding additional water, if necessary. Drizzle icing over pastries.

Kid-Friendly Baking

Excite the kids with these sweets and treats—or better yet, get them involved in the baking! Whether it's Magical Cookie Wands or Frozen Fudge Pops, everyone's sure to have a great time.

Surprise Prize Cupcakes

Makes 2 dozen cupcakes

- **1 package (15.25 or 18.25 ounces) plain chocolate cake mix**
- **⅓ cup water**
- **3 large eggs**
- **⅓ cup vegetable oil**
- **1 package (16.5 ounces) NESTLÉ® TOLL HOUSE® Refrigerated Chocolate Chip Cookie Bar Dough**
- **1 container (16 ounces) prepared chocolate frosting**
- **NESTLÉ® TOLL HOUSE® Semi-Sweet Chocolate Mini Morsels**

PREHEAT oven to 350° F. Paper-line 24 muffin cups.

BEAT cake mix, water, eggs and vegetable oil in large mixer bowl on low speed for 30 seconds. Beat on medium speed for 2 minutes or until smooth. Spoon about ¼ cup batter into each prepared muffin cup, filling about two-thirds full.

CUT cookie dough into 24 pieces; roll each into a ball. Place one ball of dough in each muffin cup, pressing it to the bottom.

BAKE for 19 to 22 minutes or until top springs back when gently touched. Let stand for 15 minutes. Remove to wire rack to cool completely. Spread with frosting and sprinkle with morsels.

Brownie Fruit Pizza

1 **package (18.3 ounces)
    traditional 13×9-inch
    chewy fudge brownie mix**

⅔ **cup vegetable oil**

2 **large eggs**

¼ **cup water**

1 **cup (6 ounces) NESTLÉ®
    TOLL HOUSE® Semi-Sweet
    Chocolate Morsels, *divided***

2 **cups thawed fat-free
    whipped topping**

3 **cups fresh fruit and berries of
    choice (blueberries, sliced
    grapes, kiwi, pineapple,
    strawberries)**

¼ **cup sweetened flaked
    coconut (optional)**

PREHEAT oven to 350° F. Grease and flour 15-inch-round pizza pan or 15×10-inch jelly-roll pan.

COMBINE brownie mix, vegetable oil, eggs and water in medium bowl until blended. Stir in *¾ cup* morsels. Spread onto prepared pizza pan.

BAKE for 20 to 22 minutes or until edges are set. Remove to wire rack and cool for 3 minutes; loosen edge of brownie crust from pan with knife. Cool for 1 hour on wire rack.

SPREAD whipped topping over brownie crust. Top with fruit. Sprinkle with *remaining ¼ cup* morsels and coconut. Serve immediately or refrigerate up to 1 hour before serving.

Tips:

● ⅓ cup unsweetened applesauce can be substituted for the vegetable oil. Bake at 350° F for 15 to 17 minutes.

● Brownie crust may be made in advance. Allow to cool completely and cover with plastic wrap for up to 1 day.

Frozen Fudge Pops

1 can (12 ounces) NESTLÉ® CARNATION® Evaporated Milk

¾ cup water

1 cup (6 ounces) NESTLÉ® TOLL HOUSE® Milk Chocolate Morsels

10 (3-ounce) paper cups

10 wooden craft sticks*

*Found in cake decorating or hobby shops.

MICROWAVE evaporated milk and water in medium, uncovered, microwave-safe bowl on HIGH (100%) power for 2 minutes or until mixture is very hot but not boiling. Add morsels; whisk until smooth.

CAREFULLY POUR about ⅓ cup chocolate mixture into each cup. Cover each cup with foil. Insert one stick through the center of each foil.

FREEZE for 4 hours or until firm. To remove pops from cups, carefully run warm water over side of cup to loosen. Peel off cup and enjoy. Freeze no longer than 1 month.

Note:

Frozen treat molds can be used. Yield may vary.

Variation:

For a richer, chocolate flavor, substitute 1 cup (6 ounces) NESTLÉ® TOLL HOUSE® Semi-Sweet Chocolate Morsels for the milk chocolate morsels.

Crazy Dipped Pretzel Rods

Makes 16 rods

1 **cup (6 ounces) NESTLÉ® TOLL HOUSE® Semi-Sweet Chocolate, Milk Chocolate or Premier White Morsels**

1 **tablespoon vegetable shortening**

16 **pretzel rods**

NESTLÉ® TOLL HOUSE® Semi-Sweet Chocolate Mini Morsels and/or sprinkles (optional)

Additional NESTLÉ® TOLL HOUSE® Morsels for drizzling (optional)

LINE baking sheet with wax paper.

MICROWAVE 1 cup morsels and vegetable shortening in small, dry, uncovered, microwave-safe bowl on MEDIUM-HIGH (70%) power for 1 minute; STIR. Morsels may retain some of their original shape. If necessary, microwave at additional 10- to 15-second intervals, stirring just until morsels are melted.

DIP pretzel rods about 3 inches into melted morsels, tilting bowl to easily dip. Use side of bowl to remove excess. Sprinkle with morsels or sprinkles. Place on prepared baking sheet. Refrigerate for 20 minutes or until set. Store in airtight container at room temperature. Best when eaten within a few days.

For a Fancy Drizzle:

Microwave 2 tablespoons of *each* desired morsel flavor in small, *heavy-duty* plastic bags on MEDIUM-HIGH (70%) power for 30 seconds; knead. Microwave at additional 10- to 15-second intervals, kneading until smooth. Cut tiny corner from each bag; squeeze to drizzle over already dipped pretzels on baking sheet. Refrigerate and store as directed above.

Peanut Butter & Chocolate Cookie Cups

Makes 3 dozen cookie cups

¾ cup (1½ sticks) butter or margarine, softened

⅓ cup granulated sugar

1½ cups all-purpose flour

1⅔ cups (11-ounce package) NESTLÉ® TOLL HOUSE® Peanut Butter & Milk Chocolate Morsels, *divided*

2 large eggs

1 can (14 ounces) NESTLÉ® CARNATION® Sweetened Condensed Milk

1 teaspoon vanilla extract

PREHEAT oven to 350° F. Heavily grease 36 mini-muffin cups.

BEAT butter and sugar in small mixer bowl until creamy. Add flour; beat until mixture is evenly moist and crumbly. Roll rounded teaspoon dough into ball; press onto bottom and halfway up side of muffin cup. Repeat with remaining dough. Place *5 morsels* in each cup.

BEAT eggs in medium bowl with wire whisk. Stir in sweetened condensed milk and vanilla extract. Spoon into muffin cups, filling almost to the top of each cup.

BAKE for 15 to 18 minutes or until centers are puffed and edges are just beginning to brown. Remove from oven to wire racks. Gently run knife around edges of cookies. Let centers flatten. While still warm, top cookies with *half of remaining morsels* (they will soften and retain their shape). Repeat with *remaining morsels*. Cool completely in pan on wire racks. With tip of knife, release cookies from cups.

Kite Cookies

Makes 20 cookies

1 package (16.5 ounces) NESTLÉ® TOLL HOUSE® Refrigerated Chocolate Chip Cookie Bar Dough

2 tablespoons all-purpose flour *plus* additional for rolling

3-inch kite or diamond cookie cutter

Assorted decorator icings, sugars and sprinkles

Thin string licorice or other rope-type candy

PREHEAT oven to 350° F.

BREAK dough apart into medium bowl. Combine dough and flour until mixed. Roll cookie dough to ¼-inch thickness between two sheets of floured wax paper. Remove top piece of paper. Cut cookie dough into kites with cutter. Transfer kites to ungreased baking sheets, placing about 4 inches apart (2 to 3 baking sheets will be needed, pending size of sheet–kites will spread). Refrigerate for 15 minutes.

BAKE for 13 to 14 minutes or until lightly browned. Remove from oven and immediately pat sides of each kite with edge of knife to help retain shape. Cool on baking sheets for 5 minutes; remove to wire racks to cool completely.

DECORATE as desired. Adhere licorice strings to kites with icing.

Tip:

Refrigerating kites before baking helps to prevent cookies from spreading and retain their shape during baking.

Easy No-Bake BUTTERFINGER® & Peanut Butter Pretzel Bars

Makes 2 dozen bars

Nonstick cooking spray

4 cups miniature marshmallows

¼ cup (½ stick) butter

¼ teaspoon salt

1¾ cups (11.5-ounce package) NESTLÉ® TOLL HOUSE® Milk Chocolate Morsels, *divided*

2 tablespoons creamy peanut butter

4 cups toasted rice cereal squares

10 (about 1½ cups) Fun Size NESTLÉ® BUTTERFINGER® Candy Bars, coarsely chopped

1 cup small pretzel twists, broken into ½-inch pieces

LINE 13×9-inch baking pan with foil leaving an overhang on two sides. Spray foil with nonstick cooking spray.

HEAT marshmallows, butter and salt in large, *heavy-duty* saucepan over medium-low heat, stirring frequently, for 5 to 10 minutes, until smooth. Remove from heat. Add *1 cup* morsels and peanut butter; stir until melted.

WORKING QUICKLY, stir in cereal, chopped Butterfinger and pretzels. Stir in *remaining ¾ cup* morsels. Spread mixture into prepared baking pan with greased spatula, pressing down lightly. Cool for 2 hours or until set. Lift from pan; remove foil. Cut into bars with serrated knife.

Magical Cookie Wands

1 package (16.5 ounces) NESTLÉ® TOLL HOUSE® Refrigerated Chocolate Chip Cookie Bar Dough

2 tablespoons all-purpose flour plus additional for rolling

12 pretzel rods

1 3-inch star cookie cutter

½ cup NESTLÉ® TOLL HOUSE® Morsels (Premier White, Semi-Sweet Chocolate, Milk Chocolate)

Decorator sugars or sprinkles (optional)

Thin ribbons (optional)

PREHEAT oven to 350° F.

BREAK dough apart into medium bowl. Combine dough and flour until mixed. Roll cookie dough to ¼-inch thickness between two sheets of floured wax paper. Remove top piece of paper. Cut cookie dough into stars with cutter. Transfer stars to baking sheet placing about 4 inches apart (2 to 3 baking sheets will be needed, pending size of sheet–stars will spread). Place pretzel rod under each star (make sure to have rod at least to middle of star or close to top). Press down lightly. Refrigerate for 15 minutes.

BAKE for 13 to 14 minutes or until lightly browned. Remove from oven and immediately pat sides of each star with edge of knife to help retain shape. Cool on baking sheets for 5 minutes; remove to wire racks to cool completely.

To Decorate:

Microwave morsels on MEDIUM-HIGH (70%) power for 30 seconds in small, *heavy-duty* plastic bag; knead. Microwave at additional 10- to 15-second intervals, kneading until smooth. Cut a small corner from bag. Squeeze bag to drizzle melted morsels over cookie stars in design desired. Immediately sprinkle with sugar or sprinkles. Let stand for 15 minutes to set drizzles.

Tip:

Refrigerating cookie wands before baking helps to prevent cookies from spreading and retain their shape during baking.

S'more Brownies

Nonstick cooking spray

9 broken in half (18 pieces) whole graham crackers, *divided*

1 package (18.3 ounces) traditional 13×9-inch chewy fudge brownie mix

¼ cup water

⅔ cup vegetable oil

2 large eggs

2 cups (12-ounce package) NESTLÉ® TOLL HOUSE® Semi-Sweet Chocolate Morsels, *divided*

2 cups miniature marshmallows

PREHEAT oven to 350° F.

LINE 13×9-inch metal baking pan with foil leaving an overhang on two sides. Spray foil with nonstick cooking spray.

PLACE *15* graham cracker halves into bottom of pan, overlapping slightly. Break *remaining* graham cracker halves into ½-inch pieces; set aside.

COMBINE brownie mix, water, vegetable oil and eggs in medium bowl until blended. Stir in *1 cup* morsels. Spread over graham crackers in pan.

BAKE for 25 to 30 minutes or until wooden pick inserted in centers comes out still slightly sticky; remove from oven.

PREHEAT broiler.

SPRINKLE *remaining* graham cracker pieces and marshmallows over warm brownies. Broil for 30 to 45 seconds or until marshmallows are light brown. Watch carefully as browning occurs very fast! A handheld kitchen butane torch can be used as well. Remove from oven to wire rack. Sprinkle immediately with *remaining 1 cup* morsels.

COOL for at least 1 hour at room temperature. Lift out by foil edges to cutting board. Carefully remove foil. Cut into bars with wet knife. Store in tightly covered container.

NESTLÉ® Graham Dippers

Makes 8 servings (2 dippers per serving)

Wax paper

3 to 4 tablespoons candy sprinkles, NESTLÉ® TOLL HOUSE® Semi-Sweet Chocolate Mini Morsels or chopped nuts

⅓ cup NESTLÉ® TOLL HOUSE® Premier White Morsels or Semi-Sweet Chocolate Mini Morsels

16 honey or cinnamon graham sticks

LINE tray with wax paper. Place candy sprinkles on plate or in shallow bowl.

MELT morsels according to package directions in small bowl. Dip one graham stick halfway into melted morsels, then into candy sprinkles. Transfer to prepared tray. Repeat with *remaining* graham sticks.

REFRIGERATE for 10 minutes or until set. Store in airtight container at room temperature for up to 1 week.

Spring S'more Bars

Makes 16 bars

½ cup heavy whipping cream

1¾ cups (11.5-ounce package) **NESTLÉ® TOLL HOUSE® Milk Chocolate Morsels**

3½ cups miniature colored marshmallows

7½ ounces chocolate-covered graham crackers, broken into bite-size pieces

LINE 9-inch-square baking pan with heavy-duty foil.

HEAT cream in medium saucepan over medium-high heat for 1 to 2 minutes or until bubbles appear around edges. Remove from heat. Add morsels; stir until smooth. Cool, stirring occasionally, for 10 to 12 minutes. Add marshmallows; stir to coat. Gently stir in graham cracker pieces until combined.

SPREAD mixture into prepared pan; press down lightly. Refrigerate for 2 hours or until firm. Cut into bars.

Mini Dessert Burgers

Makes 24 servings

1 **box (12 ounces) vanilla wafer cookies,*** *divided*

½ **cup powdered sugar**

¼ **teaspoon salt**

¾ **cup NESTLÉ® TOLL HOUSE® Semi-Sweet Chocolate Morsels**

⅓ **cup milk**

½ **cup sweetened flaked coconut**

½ **teaspoon water**

3 **drops green food coloring**

Red and yellow decorating gels (for ketchup and mustard)

1 **teaspoon melted butter (optional)**

1 **tablespoon sesame seeds (optional)**

*A 12-ounce box of vanilla wafers contains about 88 wafers.

RESERVE *48* wafers for bun tops and bottoms.

PLACE *remaining* wafers in large resealable bag. Crush into small pieces using a rolling pin. Combine wafer crumbs (about 1½ cups) with powdered sugar and salt in medium bowl.

MICROWAVE morsels and milk in medium, uncovered, microwave-safe bowl on HIGH (100%) power for 45 seconds; STIR. If necessary, microwave at additional 10- to 15-second intervals, stirring just until smooth.

POUR chocolate mixture into wafer mixture; stir until combined. Cool for 10 minutes. Line baking sheet with wax paper. Roll mixture into 24, 1-inch (about 1 tablespoonful each) balls. Place each ball on prepared sheet; flatten slightly to form burger patties.

COMBINE coconut, water and green food coloring in small, resealable plastic bag. Seal bag and shake to coat evenly with color.

TO ASSEMBLE

PLACE *24* wafers, rounded side down on prepared baking sheet. Top *each* wafer with 1 burger patty. Top *each* burger patty with 1 teaspoon colored coconut. Squeeze decorating gels on top of coconut. Top with *remaining* wafers. Brush tops of wafers with melted butter and sprinkle with sesame seeds, if desired.

Tips:

- Recipe can easily be doubled or tripled. Great birthday or slumber party activity.

- Cut apricot fruit rollups into small ½-inch squares to create cheese for the mini burgers.

NESTLÉ® TOLL HOUSE® Cookie Puzzle

Makes 24 servings

1 tub (36 ounces) NESTLÉ®
   TOLL HOUSE® Refrigerated
   Chocolate Chip Cookie Tub
   Dough*

Frosting, colored decorator
   icing, assorted NESTLÉ®
   candies and/or sprinkles,
   NESTLÉ® TOLL HOUSE®
   Morsels, any flavor

*Two packages (16.5 ounces each) NESTLÉ® TOLL
HOUSE® Refrigerated Chocolate Chip Cookie Bar
Dough can be substituted for the Tub Dough.*

PREHEAT oven to 325° F. Foil-line 15×10-inch jelly-roll pan, allowing 1-inch of foil to hang over sides of pan. Grease foil.

PLACE whole tub of dough in prepared pan. Allow to soften for 5 to 10 minutes. Using fingertips, gently press dough to evenly fill pan.

BAKE for 25 to 30 minutes or until golden brown and edges are set. Cool completely in pan on wire rack. Carefully lift from pan using foil handles to cutting board. Carefully remove foil; return to cutting board.

CUT cookie bar into 24, 2- to 4-inch random shaped pieces with pizza cutter or sharp knife. Leave pieces on cutting board, return pieces to baking sheet or place pieces on platter.

DECORATE puzzle as desired. Allow icing to set. Carefully separate using knife into individual puzzle pieces.

Tip:

Puzzle may be decorated for a variety of holidays or occasions.

Peanut Butter and Jelly Bars

Makes 4 dozen bars

1¼ cups all-purpose flour

½ cup graham cracker crumbs

½ teaspoon baking soda

½ teaspoon salt

½ cup (1 stick) butter, softened

½ cup packed brown sugar

½ cup granulated sugar

½ cup creamy peanut butter

1 large egg

1 teaspoon vanilla extract

1¾ cups (11.5-ounce package)
  NESTLÉ® TOLL HOUSE®
  Milk Chocolate Morsels

¾ cup coarsely chopped
  peanuts

½ cup jelly or jam

PREHEAT oven to 350° F.

COMBINE flour, graham cracker crumbs, baking soda and salt in small bowl.

BEAT butter, brown sugar, granulated sugar and peanut butter in large mixer bowl until creamy. Beat in egg and vanilla extract. Gradually beat in flour mixture. Stir in morsels and nuts. Press ¾ *dough* into ungreased 13×9-inch baking pan.

BAKE for 15 minutes; remove from oven. Dollop jelly by heaping teaspoon over partially baked dough. Let stand for 1 minute; spread to cover. Dollop *remaining* dough by heaping teaspoon over jelly.

BAKE for an additional 20 to 25 minutes or until edges are set. Cool in pan on wire rack. Cut into bars.

PB+J bars

Kids' Favorite Chocolate Chip Muffins

Makes 3 dozen muffins

1½ **cups all-purpose flour**

1½ **cups whole-wheat flour**

2 **teaspoons baking soda**

2 **teaspoons baking powder**

2 **teaspoons ground cinnamon or pumpkin pie spice**

½ **teaspoon salt**

4 **large eggs, slightly beaten**

2 **cups granulated sugar**

1 **can (15 ounces) LIBBY'S® 100% Pure Pumpkin**

1 **cup vegetable oil**

2 **cups (12-ounce package) NESTLÉ® TOLL HOUSE® Semi-Sweet Chocolate Morsels**

PREHEAT oven to 350° F. Grease thirty-six 2½-inch muffin cups or line with paper bake cups.

COMBINE all-purpose flour, whole-wheat flour, baking soda, baking powder, cinnamon and salt in medium bowl. Combine eggs and sugar in large bowl. Add pumpkin and oil; mix well. Stir in flour mixture until moistened. Stir in morsels. Spoon batter into prepared muffin cups.

BAKE for 20 to 25 minutes or until top springs back when lightly touched. Cool in pans on wire racks for 5 minutes; remove from pans.

NESTLÉ® TOLL HOUSE® Hot Cocoa

Makes 4 servings

½ **cup granulated sugar**

⅓ **cup NESTLÉ® TOLL HOUSE®**
   Baking Cocoa

4 **cups milk, *divided***

1 **teaspoon vanilla extract**

Whipped cream or miniature
marshmallows (optional)

COMBINE sugar and cocoa in medium saucepan; stir. Gradually stir in ⅓ *cup* milk to make a smooth paste; stir in *remaining* milk.

WARM over medium heat, stirring constantly, until hot (do not boil). Remove from heat; stir in vanilla extract. Top with whipped cream or marshmallows, if desired, before serving.

Kid-Friendly Baking   141

Very Best Brownies & Bars

Whether you're entertaining a crowd or cooking for a few, these delectable baked bars, rich chocolate brownies, and sweet-and-salty snacks are the perfect way to show someone you care at any time.

Scrumptious Chocolate Mint Layer Bars

Makes 2 dozen bars

¼ cup (½ stick) butter or margarine

2 cups (about 15) finely ground crème-filled chocolate sandwich cookies

1½ cups chopped nuts

1 cup flaked coconut

1 can (14 ounces) NESTLÉ® CARNATION® Sweetened Condensed Milk

1⅔ cups (10-ounce package) NESTLÉ® TOLL HOUSE® Dark Chocolate & Mint Morsels

PREHEAT oven to 350° F.

MELT butter in 13×9-inch baking pan in oven; remove from oven. Sprinkle cookie crumbs over butter. Stir well; press mixture onto bottom of pan. Sprinkle with nuts and coconut. Pour sweetened condensed milk evenly over top. Sprinkle with morsels; press down slightly.

BAKE for 20 to 25 minutes or until coconut is light golden brown. Cool completely in pan on wire rack. Cut into bars.

Chocolate Cherry Merlot Brownies

1¼ cups (6-ounce package) dried sweet cherries,* chopped

½ cup Merlot wine

2 bars (8 ounces) NESTLÉ® TOLL HOUSE® Dark Chocolate Baking Bar, broken into small pieces

1⅓ cups all-purpose flour

½ teaspoon salt

1 cup granulated sugar

⅓ cup butter, softened

2 large eggs

1 teaspoon vanilla extract

Sweetened dried cranberries can be substituted for the dried cherries.

PREHEAT oven to 350° F. Grease 9-inch square baking pan.

MICROWAVE dried cherries and wine in small, uncovered, microwave-safe bowl on HIGH (100%) power for 1 minute. Set aside for 15 minutes, stirring occasionally. Drain cherries; discard wine.

MICROWAVE chocolate in small, uncovered, microwave-safe bowl on HIGH (100%) power for 45 seconds; STIR. If pieces retain some of their original shape, microwave at additional 10- to 15-second intervals, stirring just until melted; cool to room temperature.

COMBINE flour and salt in small bowl. Beat sugar and butter in medium mixer bowl until well mixed. Add eggs and beat until light and fluffy. Beat in melted chocolate and vanilla extract. Stir in flour mixture until blended. Stir in drained cherries. Spread into prepared pan.

BAKE for 33 to 37 minutes or until wooden pick inserted in center comes out slightly sticky. Cool completely in pan on wire rack. Cut into bars.

Razz-Ma-Tazz Bars

Makes 16 bars

½ **cup (1 stick) butter or margarine**

2 **cups (12-ounce package) NESTLÉ® TOLL HOUSE® Premier White Morsels, divided**

2 **large eggs**

½ **cup granulated sugar**

1 **cup all-purpose flour**

½ **teaspoon salt**

½ **teaspoon almond extract**

½ **cup seedless raspberry jam**

¼ **cup toasted sliced almonds**

PREHEAT oven to 325° F. Grease and sugar 9-inch-square baking pan.

MELT butter in medium, microwave-safe bowl on HIGH (100%) power for 1 minute; stir. Add *1 cup* morsels; let stand. Do not stir.

BEAT eggs in large mixer bowl until foamy. Add sugar; beat until light lemon colored, about 5 minutes. Stir in morsel-butter mixture. Add flour, salt and almond extract; mix at low speed until combined. Spread ⅔ of batter into prepared pan.

BAKE for 15 to 17 minutes or until light golden brown around edges. Remove from oven to wire rack.

HEAT jam in small, microwave-safe bowl on HIGH (100%) power for 30 seconds; stir. Spread jam over warm crust. Stir *remaining 1 cup* morsels into *remaining* batter. Drop spoonfuls of batter over jam. Sprinkle with almonds.

BAKE for 25 to 30 minutes or until edges are browned. Cool completely in pan on wire rack. Cut into bars.

Tip:

To sugar a baking pan, simply sprinkle it with a tablespoon of sugar after greasing.

Milk Chocolate Banana Brownies

Makes 16 brownies

1¾ cups (11.5-ounce package) **NESTLÉ® TOLL HOUSE® Milk Chocolate Morsels,** *divided*

½ cup all-purpose flour

½ cup whole-wheat flour

¾ teaspoon baking powder

½ teaspoon salt

1 cup packed light brown sugar

½ cup (1 stick) butter, *softened*

2 large eggs

1 teaspoon vanilla extract

2 medium ripe bananas, quartered lengthwise and chopped

PREHEAT oven to 350° F. Grease 9-inch-square baking pan.

MICROWAVE *1 cup* morsels in small, uncovered, microwave-safe bowl on MEDIUM-HIGH (70%) power for 45 seconds; STIR. If necessary, microwave at additional 10- to 15-second intervals, stirring just until smooth. Cool to room temperature.

COMBINE all-purpose flour, whole-wheat flour, baking powder and salt in small bowl. Beat brown sugar and butter in medium mixer bowl until creamy. Add eggs and vanilla extract; beat well. Beat in melted chocolate. Gradually beat in flour mixture. Stir in bananas and *remaining ¾ cup* morsels. Spread into prepared baking pan.

BAKE for 40 to 45 minutes or until wooden pick inserted in center comes out clean. Cool completely in pan on wire rack. Cut into bars. Store in covered container in refrigerator.

Dark Chocolate Crumb Bars

Makes 2½ dozen bars

- ¾ cup (1½ sticks) butter, softened
- 1¾ cups all-purpose flour
- ⅓ cup granulated sugar
- ¼ teaspoon salt
- 1⅔ cups (10-ounce package) NESTLÉ® TOLL HOUSE® Dark Chocolate Morsels, *divided*
- 1 can (14 ounces) NESTLÉ® CARNATION® Sweetened Condensed Milk
- 1 teaspoon vanilla extract
- 1 cup chopped walnuts (optional)

PREHEAT oven to 350° F. Grease 13×9-inch baking pan.

BEAT butter in large mixer bowl until creamy. Beat in flour, sugar and salt until crumbly. With floured fingers, press *2 cups* crumb mixture onto bottom of prepared baking pan; reserve *remaining* mixture.

BAKE for 10 to 12 minutes or until edges are golden brown.

COMBINE *1 cup* morsels and sweetened condensed milk in small, *heavy-duty* saucepan. Warm over low heat, stirring until smooth. Stir in vanilla extract. Spread over hot crust.

STIR nuts and *remaining ⅔ cup* morsels into reserved crumb mixture; sprinkle over chocolate filling.

BAKE for 25 to 30 minutes or until center is set. Cool in pan on wire rack. Cut into bars.

Chocolatey Peanut Pretzel Bars

Makes 2 dozen bars

2½ cups NESTLÉ® TOLL HOUSE® Refrigerated Chocolate Chip Cookie Tub Dough, *divided*

1½ cups (9 ounces) NESTLÉ® TOLL HOUSE® Semi-Sweet Chocolate Morsels, *divided*

1 cup mini-pretzels (about 1¼ ounces), broken into ½-inch pieces

1 cup honey-roasted peanuts

PREHEAT oven to 350° F. Grease 13×9-inch baking pan.

PLACE *2 cups* dough in prepared pan. Using fingertips, pat dough gently to cover bottom.

SPRINKLE *1 cup* morsels, pretzel pieces and peanuts over dough. Drop 1-inch pieces of *remaining ½ cup* cookie dough over peanuts. Sprinkle with *remaining ½ cup* of morsels and gently press down.

BAKE for 23 to 27 minutes or until browned around edges. Cool completely in pan on wire rack. Cut into bars.

Sweet & Salty Chewy Pecan Bars

Makes 16 servings

1 **package (16.5 ounces) NESTLÉ® TOLL HOUSE® Refrigerated Chocolate Chip Cookie Bar Dough, divided**

1 **tablespoon butter, melted**

¾ **cup chopped pecans**

1 **tablespoon granulated sugar**

¼ **teaspoon salt**

⅓ **cup NESTLÉ® TOLL HOUSE® Semi-Sweet Chocolate Morsels**

2 **tablespoons caramel sauce**

PREHEAT oven to 350° F. Grease 8-inch-square baking pan.

PRESS *¾ package* (18 squares) cookie dough into prepared baking pan and refrigerate *remaining ¼ package* (6 squares) cookie dough.

BAKE for 10 minutes; remove from oven.

COMBINE butter, nuts, sugar and salt in small bowl until coated. Sprinkle over dough. Top with teaspoonfuls of *remaining* cookie dough; pressing down gently. Sprinkle with morsels.

BAKE for an additional 22 to 24 minutes or until edges are browned and set. Cool 30 minutes in pan on wire rack.

DRIZZLE caramel sauce over bar. Cool completely in pan on wire rack. Cut into bars.

Tips:

● For chewier caramel top, microwave 6 unwrapped caramel candies with 1 teaspoon milk for 20 to 30 seconds or until melted; stir until smooth. Drizzle sauce over bar.

● Toasted pecans may also be used, if desired.

Premier Cheesecake Cranberry Bars

2 **cups all-purpose flour**

1½ **cups quick or old-fashioned oats**

¼ **cup packed light brown sugar**

1 **cup (2 sticks) butter or margarine, softened**

2 **cups (12-ounce package) NESTLÉ® TOLL HOUSE® Premier White Morsels**

1 **package (8 ounces) cream cheese, softened**

1 **can (14 ounces) NESTLÉ® CARNATION® Sweetened Condensed Milk**

¼ **cup lemon juice**

1 **teaspoon vanilla extract**

1 **can (14 ounces) whole-berry cranberry sauce**

2 **tablespoons cornstarch**

PREHEAT oven to 350° F. Grease 13×9-inch baking pan.

COMBINE flour, oats and brown sugar in large bowl. Add butter; mix until crumbly. Stir in morsels. Reserve *2½ cups* morsel mixture for topping. With floured fingers, press *remaining* mixture into prepared pan.

BEAT cream cheese in large mixer bowl until creamy. Add sweetened condensed milk, lemon juice and vanilla extract; mix until smooth. Pour over crust. Combine cranberry sauce and cornstarch in medium bowl. Spoon over cream cheese mixture. Sprinkle *reserved* morsel mixture over cranberry mixture.

BAKE for 35 to 40 minutes or until center is set. Cool completely in pan on wire rack. Cover; refrigerate until serving time (up to 1 day). Cut into bars.

Minty-Licious Ice Cream Freeze

Makes 15 servings

12 **chocolate graham crackers, finely ground (about 1½ cups)**

½ **cup (1 stick) butter or margarine, melted**

1⅔ **cups (10-ounce package) NESTLÉ® TOLL HOUSE® Dark Chocolate & Mint Morsels, *divided***

1 **cup broken-up mini-pretzels (about 40), *divided***

1 **container (1.5 quarts) Chocolate or Vanilla DREYER'S or EDY'S® SLOW CHURNED® Light Ice Cream, slightly softened**

NESTLÉ® NESQUIK® Chocolate Flavor Syrup (optional)

LINE 13×9-inch baking pan with plastic wrap or foil with edges hanging over sides.

MIX crumbs and butter in small bowl. Press onto bottom of prepared pan. Sprinkle *1 cup* morsels and *½ cup* pretzels over crumb crust. Scoop ice cream over morsels; spread evenly with knife or small spatula.

SPRINKLE with *remaining ⅔ cup* morsels and *½ cup* pretzels; press down lightly. Freeze for at least 2 hours.

TO SERVE: Let stand for 5 minutes. Lift dessert out of pan; remove plastic wrap. Cut into squares. Drizzle each serving with Nesquik.

Layers of Love Chocolate Brownies

Makes 16 brownies

¾ cup all-purpose flour

¾ cup NESTLÉ® TOLL HOUSE® Baking Cocoa

¼ teaspoon salt

½ cup (1 stick) butter, cut into pieces

½ cup granulated sugar

½ cup packed brown sugar

3 large eggs, *divided*

2 teaspoons vanilla extract

1 cup chopped pecans

¾ cup NESTLÉ® TOLL HOUSE® Premier White Morsels

½ cup caramel ice cream topping

¾ cup NESTLÉ® TOLL HOUSE® Semi-Sweet Chocolate Morsels

PREHEAT oven to 350° F. Grease 8-inch-square baking pan.

COMBINE flour, cocoa and salt in small bowl. Beat butter, granulated sugar and brown sugar in large mixer bowl until creamy. Add *2 eggs,* one at a time, beating well after each addition. Add vanilla extract; mix well. Gradually beat in flour mixture. Reserve ¾ *cup* batter. Spread *remaining* batter into prepared baking pan. Sprinkle nuts and white morsels over batter. Drizzle caramel topping over top. Beat *remaining* egg and *reserved* batter in same large bowl until light in color. Stir in semi-sweet morsels. Spread evenly over caramel topping.

BAKE for 30 to 35 minutes or until center is set. Cool completely in pan on wire rack. Cut into squares.

Citrus-Iced Mock Margarita Bars

Makes 16 bars

BAR

- 1 cup *plus* 2 tablespoons all-purpose flour
- 1 teaspoon baking powder
- ¼ teaspoon salt
- ¾ cup granulated sugar
- ⅓ cup butter, softened
- ½ teaspoon vanilla extract
- 2 teaspoons grated lime peel
- 2 teaspoons grated orange peel
- 1 large egg
- 1 cup (6 ounces) NESTLÉ® TOLL HOUSE® Premier White Morsels

CITRUS ICING

- 1½ cups sifted powdered sugar
- 4 ounces cream cheese, at room temperature
- 1 tablespoon butter, softened
- 1 teaspoon grated lime peel
- 1 teaspoon grated orange peel
- 2 teaspoons lime juice
- 1 teaspoon orange juice
- 1 to 2 teaspoons coarse sea salt (optional)

FOR BARS

PREHEAT oven to 350° F. Grease 9-inch-square baking pan.

COMBINE flour, baking powder and salt in small bowl. Beat sugar, butter, vanilla extract, lime peel and orange peel in large mixer bowl until creamy. Beat in egg. Gradually beat in flour mixture. Stir in morsels. Press into prepared baking pan.

BAKE for 18 to 20 minutes or until wooden pick inserted in center comes out clean. Cool completely in pan on wire rack. Spread with Citrus Icing. Sprinkle with sea salt. Cut into bars. Store in covered container in refrigerator.

FOR CITRUS ICING

BEAT powdered sugar, cream cheese, butter, lime peel, orange peel, lime juice and orange juice in small mixer bowl until smooth.

Tip:

Bars can be prepared in an 8-inch-square baking pan. Follow recipe above and bake for 20 to 22 minutes.

Flourless Chocolate Brownies

Makes 16 brownies

2 cups (12-ounce package) **NESTLÉ® TOLL HOUSE®** **Semi-Sweet Chocolate Morsels**, *divided*

¾ cup (1½ sticks) **butter**, cut into pieces

2 tablespoons **water**

¼ cup **NESTLÉ® TOLL HOUSE® Baking Cocoa**

4 large **eggs**

⅓ cup **granulated sugar**

1 teaspoon **vanilla extract**

1 cup **pecans, finely ground (optional)**

¼ cup **heavy whipping cream**

PREHEAT oven to 300° F. Line 9-inch-square baking pan with foil. Grease bottom and sides.

HEAT *1½ cups* morsels, butter and water in medium, *heavy-duty* saucepan over low heat, stirring constantly, until morsels and butter are melted and mixture is smooth. Stir in cocoa until smooth. Remove from heat.

BEAT eggs and sugar in medium mixer bowl until thick, about 4 minutes. Stir in vanilla extract. Fold ⅓ of egg mixture into chocolate mixture. Fold in *remaining* egg mixture, one half at a time, until thoroughly incorporated. Fold in pecans. Pour into prepared pan.

BAKE for 35 to 40 minutes or until risen in center and edges start to get firm and shiny (center may still move and appear underbaked). Cool completely in pan on wire rack (center may sink slightly). Cover; refrigerate for 4 hours or overnight.

PLACE cream in small, uncovered, microwave-safe dish. Microwave on HIGH (100%) power for 25 to 30 seconds. Add *remaining ½ cup* morsels. Let stand for 2 to 3 minutes; stir until chocolate is melted.

SPREAD ganache over chilled brownie. Refrigerate for 30 minutes. Using two opposite sides of foil, carefully lift the entire brownie out of the pan and place on cutting board. Carefully peel away foil from brownie. Cut into bars. Store in tightly covered container in refrigerator.

Chocolate Amaretto Bars

CRUST

- **2 cups all-purpose flour**
- **¾ cup (1½ sticks) butter or margarine, cut into pieces, softened**
- **⅓ cup packed brown sugar**

FILLING

- **4 large eggs**
- **¾ cup light corn syrup**
- **¾ cup granulated sugar**
- **2 tablespoons butter or margarine, melted**
- **1 tablespoon cornstarch**
- **¼ cup amaretto liqueur *or* ½ teaspoon almond extract**
- **2 cups sliced almonds**
- **2 cups (12-ounce package) NESTLÉ® TOLL HOUSE® Semi-Sweet Chocolate Morsels, *divided***
- **Chocolate Drizzle (recipe follows)**

PREHEAT oven to 350° F. Grease 13×9-inch baking pan.

FOR CRUST

BEAT flour, butter and brown sugar in large mixer bowl until crumbly. Press into prepared baking pan.

BAKE for 12 to 15 minutes or until golden brown.

FOR FILLING

BEAT eggs, corn syrup, granulated sugar, butter, cornstarch and liqueur in medium bowl with wire whisk. Stir in almonds and *1⅔ cups* morsels. Pour over hot crust; spread evenly.

BAKE for 25 to 30 minutes or until center is set. Cool in pan on wire rack.

Chocolate Drizzle: PLACE *remaining ⅓ cup* morsels in *heavy-duty* plastic bag. Microwave on HIGH (100%) power for 30 to 45 seconds; knead. Microwave at 10- to 15-second intervals, kneading until smooth. Cut tiny corner from bag; squeeze to drizzle over bars. Refrigerate for a few minutes to firm chocolate before cutting into bars.

Irish Coffee Brownies

Makes 16 brownies

2¾ cups (11.5-ounce package) **NESTLÉ® TOLL HOUSE® Milk Chocolate Morsels,** *divided*

½ **cup (1 stick) butter**

½ **cup granulated sugar**

2 **large eggs**

1 **teaspoon vanilla extract**

2 **teaspoons Irish whiskey***

2 **teaspoons NESCAFÉ® TASTER'S CHOICE® House Blend 100% Pure Instant Coffee Granules**

1 **cup all-purpose flour**

2 **tablespoons water**

*An additional 1½ teaspoons of vanilla extract plus 4½ teaspoons water can be substituted for the Irish whiskey.

PREHEAT oven to 350° F. Grease 8-inch-square baking pan.

MELT *1 cup* morsels and butter in small saucepan over low heat, stirring occasionally until morsels are melted and mixture is smooth. Remove from heat; cool to room temperature, about 15 minutes.

WHISK sugar and eggs in large bowl until thick and lemon colored. Gradually beat in chocolate mixture and vanilla extract. Combine whiskey and coffee granules in small cup; stir until dissolved. Add to chocolate mixture. Gradually stir in flour. Pour into prepared pan.

BAKE for 25 to 30 minutes or until wooden pick inserted in center comes out clean. Immediately sprinkle with remaining ¾ cup morsels. Let stand for 5 minutes or until morsels are shiny and soft; spread evenly. Cool completely in pan on wire rack. Cut into squares.

Chocolate Chip Cranberry Cheese Bars

1 **cup (2 sticks) butter or margarine, softened**

1 **cup firmly packed brown sugar**

2 **cups all-purpose flour**

1½ **cups quick or old-fashioned oats**

2 **teaspoons grated orange peel**

2 **cups (12-ounce package) NESTLÉ® TOLL HOUSE® Semi-Sweet Chocolate Morsels**

1 **cup dried cranberries**

1 **package (8 ounces) cream cheese, softened**

1 **can (14 ounces) NESTLÉ® CARNATION® Sweetened Condensed Milk**

PREHEAT oven to 350° F. Grease 13×9-inch baking pan.

BEAT butter and brown sugar in large mixer bowl until creamy. Gradually beat in flour, oats and orange peel until crumbly. Stir in morsels and cranberries; reserve *2 cups* mixture. Press *remaining* mixture onto bottom of prepared baking pan.

BAKE for 15 minutes. Beat cream cheese in small mixer bowl until smooth. Gradually beat in sweetened condensed milk. Pour over hot crust; sprinkle with reserved flour mixture. Bake for additional 25 to 30 minutes or until center is set. Cool in pan on wire rack. Cut into bars.

Dark Chocolate Brownies

Makes 16 brownies

1⅔ cups (10-ounce package) **NESTLÉ® TOLL HOUSE® Dark Chocolate Morsels,** *divided*

1 cup granulated sugar

⅓ cup butter, cut into pieces

2 tablespoons water

2 large eggs

1 teaspoon vanilla extract

¾ cup all-purpose flour

¼ teaspoon salt

½ cup chopped walnuts or pecans (optional)

PREHEAT oven to 325° F. Grease 8-inch-square baking pan. Set aside ⅓ *cup* morsels.

HEAT *1⅓ cups* morsels, sugar, butter and water in small saucepan over low heat, stirring constantly, until chocolate and butter are melted. Pour into medium bowl. Stir in eggs, one at a time, with wire whisk until blended. Stir in vanilla extract. Add flour and salt; stir well. Stir in *reserved ⅓ cup* morsels and nuts. Pour into prepared baking pan.

BAKE for 38 to 40 minutes or until wooden pick inserted in center comes out slightly sticky. Cool in pan on wire rack. Cut into bars.

Year Round Holiday Recipes

Holiday baking made easy! Create colorful bark for Easter, cookie pops for Halloween, and a brownie torte for July 4th. You can even give homemade sweet gifts for the winter holidays this year.

Chewy Brownie Mix in a Jar

Makes 2 dozen brownies

1⅔ cups granulated sugar

¾ cup NESTLÉ® TOLL HOUSE® Baking Cocoa

1⅓ cups all-purpose flour

½ teaspoon baking powder

¼ teaspoon salt

¾ cup NESTLÉ® TOLL HOUSE® Semi-Sweet Chocolate Morsels

LAYER ingredients in order listed in 1-quart jar, pressing firmly after adding each ingredient. Be sure to wipe out inside of jar with paper towel after adding cocoa. Seal with lid and decorate with fabric and ribbon.

Recipe to Attach: PREHEAT oven to 350° F. Grease 13×9-inch baking pan. **POUR** brownie mix into large mixer bowl; stir. Add ¾ cup (1½ sticks) melted butter or margarine, 2 large eggs, 2 tablespoons water and 2 teaspoons vanilla extract; stir well. Spread into prepared baking pan. **BAKE** for 18 to 25 minutes or until wooden pick inserted in center comes out slightly sticky. Cool completely in pan on wire rack. Dust with powdered sugar. Makes 2 dozen brownies.

Chocolate Mint Truffles

Makes 48 truffles

1¾ cups (11.5-ounce package) NESTLÉ® TOLL HOUSE® Milk Chocolate Morsels

1 cup (6 ounces) NESTLÉ® TOLL HOUSE® Semi-Sweet Chocolate Morsels

¾ cup heavy whipping cream

1 tablespoon peppermint extract

1½ cups finely chopped walnuts, toasted, or NESTLÉ® TOLL HOUSE® Baking Cocoa

LINE baking sheet with wax paper.

PLACE milk chocolate and semi-sweet morsels in large mixer bowl. Heat cream to a gentle boil in small saucepan; pour over morsels. Let stand for 1 minute; stir until smooth. Stir in peppermint extract. Cover with plastic wrap; refrigerate for 35 to 45 minutes or until slightly thickened. Stir just until color lightens slightly. (*Do not* overmix or truffles will be grainy.)

DROP by rounded teaspoon onto prepared baking sheet; refrigerate for 10 to 15 minutes. Shape into balls; roll in walnuts or cocoa. Store in airtight container in refrigerator.

Variation:

After rolling chocolate mixture into balls, freeze for 30 to 40 minutes. Microwave 1¾ cups (11.5-ounce package) NESTLÉ® TOLL HOUSE® Milk Chocolate Morsels and 3 tablespoons vegetable shortening in medium, uncovered, microwave-safe bowl on MEDIUM-HIGH (70%) power for 1 minute; STIR. Morsels may retain some of their original shape. If necessary, microwave at additional 10- to 15-second intervals, stirring just until morsels are melted. Dip truffles into chocolate mixture; shake off excess. Place on foil-lined baking sheets. Refrigerate for 15 to 20 minutes or until set. Store in airtight container in refrigerator.

Chocolate Chip Easter Baskets

Makes 2 dozen baskets

1 **package (16.5 ounces) NESTLÉ® TOLL HOUSE® Refrigerated Chocolate Chip Cookie Bar Dough**

1 **cup prepared white frosting**

Green food coloring

¼ **cup sweetened flaked coconut**

WONKA® SweeTARTS® or SPREE® Jelly Beans

Thin-string licorice, various colors, cut into 3-inch pieces for basket handles (optional)

PREHEAT oven to 350° F. Grease and flour 24 mini-muffin cups. Place one square of cookie dough into each cup.

BAKE for 14 to 17 minutes or until golden brown. Remove pans to wire rack. If licorice handles are to be added, with tip of wooden pick, make two holes opposite each other on top edge of cup. Make sure holes are the same size as the width of the licorice. This is best done when cups are very warm. Cool cups completely in pans on wire rack. With tip of butter knife, remove cookie cups from muffin pans. Arrange on serving platter.

COMBINE frosting and a few drops of food coloring in small bowl, adding additional food coloring until desired shade is reached.

DISSOLVE a few drops of food coloring in ¼ teaspoon water in small, resealable food storage plastic bag. Add coconut. Seal bag and shake to evenly coat coconut.

SPOON a small amount of frosting onto the top of each cup. Add a pinch of tinted coconut. Top grass with SweeTARTS Jelly Beans. Insert ends of licorice into small holes in cups for handles.

Monster Pops

1⅔ cups all-purpose flour

1 teaspoon baking soda

½ teaspoon salt

1 cup (2 sticks) butter or margarine, softened

¾ cup granulated sugar

¾ cup packed brown sugar

2 teaspoons vanilla extract

2 large eggs

2 cups (12-ounce package) NESTLÉ® TOLL HOUSE® Semi-Sweet Chocolate Morsels

2 cups old-fashioned oats

1 cup raisins

24 wooden craft sticks

1 container (16 ounces) prepared vanilla frosting, colored as desired, or colored icing in tubes

PREHEAT oven to 325° F.

COMBINE flour, baking soda and salt in small bowl. Beat butter, granulated sugar, brown sugar and vanilla extract in large mixer bowl until creamy. Beat in eggs. Gradually beat in flour mixture. Stir in morsels, oats and raisins. Drop dough by level ¼-cup measure 3 inches apart onto ungreased baking sheets. Shape into round mounds. Insert wooden stick into side of each mound.

BAKE for 14 to 18 minutes or until golden brown. Cool on baking sheets on wire racks for 2 minutes; remove to wire racks to cool completely.

DECORATE pops as desired.

For Speedy Monster Pops: SUBSTITUTE 2 packages (16.5 ounce each), NESTLÉ® TOLL HOUSE® Refrigerated Chocolate Chip Cookie Dough for the first nine ingredients, adding 1 cup quick or old-fashioned oats and ½ cup raisins to the dough. Bake as stated above for 16 to 20 minutes or until golden brown. Makes 1½ dozen cookies.

Red, White and Blueberry Torte

Makes 8 to 10 servings

TORTE

- ¾ cup granulated sugar
- 6 tablespoons butter or margarine
- 1 tablespoon water
- 1½ cups (9 ounces) NESTLÉ® TOLL HOUSE® Semi-Sweet Chocolate Morsels, *divided*
- 1 teaspoon vanilla extract, *divided*
- 2 large eggs
- ⅔ cup all-purpose flour
- ¼ teaspoon baking soda
- ¼ teaspoon salt

TOPPING

- 1 package (8 ounces) cream cheese, at room temperature
- 2 tablespoons granulated sugar
- ½ of an 8-ounce container frozen light whipped topping, thawed
- 2 cups sliced strawberries
- ¼ cup fresh blueberries

FOR TORTE

PREHEAT oven to 350° F. Line 9-inch-round cake pan with wax paper; grease paper.

COMBINE *¾ cup* sugar, butter and water in small, *heavy-duty* saucepan. Bring to a boil, stirring constantly; remove from heat. Add *¾ cup* morsels; stir until smooth. Stir in *½ teaspoon* vanilla extract. Add eggs, one at a time, stirring well after each addition. Add flour, baking soda and salt; stir until well blended. Stir in *remaining ¾ cup* morsels. Pour into prepared cake pan.

BAKE for 20 to 25 minutes or until wooden pick inserted in center comes out slightly sticky. Cool in pan for 15 minutes. Invert torte onto wire rack; remove wax paper. Turn right side up; cool completely.

FOR TOPPING

BEAT cream cheese, *2 tablespoons* sugar and *remaining ½ teaspoon* vanilla extract in small mixer bowl until creamy. Stir in whipped topping. Spread over torte; top with berries. Refrigerate until ready to serve.

NESTLÉ® TOLL HOUSE® Stars and Stripes Cookies

Makes 20 cookies

1 package (16.5 ounces) NESTLÉ® TOLL HOUSE® Refrigerated Chocolate Chip Cookie Bar Dough

1 package (8 ounces) light cream cheese (Neufchâtel), at room temperature

⅓ cup granulated sugar

24 fresh, medium strawberries, sliced

¾ cup fresh blueberries

2 tablespoons NESTLÉ® TOLL HOUSE® Semi-Sweet Chocolate Mini Morsels

PREHEAT oven to 350° F.

ROLL cookie dough to ¼-inch thickness between two pieces of wax paper. Remove top piece of paper. Cut cookie dough into stars with 3-inch star cookie cutter. Transfer cookies to ungreased baking sheet(s). (If stars are too hard to remove from wax paper, refrigerate rolled dough for 10 minutes.) Roll remaining dough to ¼-inch thickness; cut out additional stars.

BAKE for 10 to 12 minutes or until light golden brown. While hot, reshape and pat edges of each star back into shape with knife. Cool on baking sheet(s) for 2 minutes; remove to wire rack(s) to cool completely.

BEAT cream cheese and sugar in small mixer bowl until fluffy. Spread onto cooled cookies. Place strawberry slices onto each cookie pointing outward. Place 5 to 6 blueberries in center of each cookie. Top each cookie with morsels.

Rich Peppermint Sipping Cocoa Mix

Makes 1 jar

1½ cups NESTLÉ® TOLL HOUSE® Semi-Sweet Chocolate Morsels

¾ cup NESTLÉ® TOLL HOUSE® Premier White Morsels

15 (about 6 tablespoons) hard peppermint candies, unwrapped and crushed into small pieces*

1 (3-cup) gifting jar with lid or 16-inch disposable plastic pastry bag with twist tie or ribbon

*To crush peppermint candies, place unwrapped candies in heavy-duty plastic bag; seal. Crush using rolling pin or other heavy object.

LAYER semi-sweet morsels, white morsels and crushed peppermint candies in gifting jar or plastic pastry bag. Seal jar with lid or tie pastry bag closed with twist tie.

Recipe to Attach: COMBINE entire contents of cocoa mix with 1 can (12 fluid ounces) NESTLÉ® CARNATION® Evaporated Milk and 1½ cups water in medium saucepan. Cook over low heat, stirring occasionally, for 10 to 12 minutes or until peppermint candy is dissolved and chocolate is melted. Makes 8, 4-ounce servings.

Tip:

The cocoa mix can be divided in half to make two mix gifts. Place mix in two smaller jars with lids or two 12-inch disposable plastic pastry bags.

Recipe to Attach: COMBINE entire contents of cocoa mix with ⅔ cup (5 fluid-ounce can) NESTLÉ® CARNATION® Evaporated Milk and 1 cup water in medium saucepan. **COOK** over low heat, stirring occasionally, for 8 to 10 minutes or until peppermint candy is dissolved and chocolate is melted. Makes 4, 4-ounce servings.

Dipped Peppermint Spoons

Makes 8 spoons

¼ cup NESTLÉ® TOLL HOUSE®
    Semi-Sweet Chocolate
    Morsels

½ teaspoon vegetable
    shortening

8 plastic spoons (for dipping
   in chocolate)

2 tablespoons NESTLÉ®
   TOLL HOUSE® Premier
   White Morsels

3 (about 1 tablespoon) hard
   peppermint candies,
   unwrapped and crushed
   into small pieces*

8 cellophane bags and
   twist ties or ribbons for
   wrapping

*To crush peppermint candies, place unwrapped
candies in heavy-duty plastic bag; seal. Crush using
rolling pin or other heavy object.*

LINE baking sheet with wax paper.

MICROWAVE semi-sweet morsels and vegetable shortening in small, uncovered, microwave-safe bowl on HIGH (100%) power for 20 seconds; STIR. Morsels may retain some of their original shape. If necessary, microwave at additional 10- to 15-second intervals, stirring just until morsels are melted.

DIP the end of *each* spoon in melted chocolate, tilting bowl to easily dip. Use side of bowl to remove excess. Place on prepared baking sheet. Refrigerate for 15 minutes or until set.

MICROWAVE white morsels in small, *heavy-duty* plastic bag on MEDIUM-HIGH (70%) power for 20 seconds; knead. Microwave at additional 10- to 15-second intervals, kneading until smooth. Cut tiny corner from each bag. Squeeze to drizzle over ends of already dipped spoons. Dip spoons in crushed peppermints; return to baking sheet. Let stand until set. Insert spoons into bags and secure with ties. Store at room temperature.

'Tis the Season Gingerbread Bark

Makes 2 dozen pieces

Parchment or wax paper

2 bars (8 ounces) NESTLÉ® TOLL HOUSE® Dark Chocolate Baking Bar,* finely chopped

¼ cup NESTLÉ® TOLL HOUSE® Premier White Morsels

1 teaspoon vegetable oil

⅓ to ½ cup chopped or crumbled gingersnap cookies

*You may substitute 1¼ cups NESTLÉ® TOLL HOUSE® Semi-Sweet Chocolate Morsels for the dark chocolate baking bars.

LINE baking sheet with parchment or wax paper.

MELT ⅔ of dark chocolate in uncovered, microwave-safe bowl on MEDIUM-HIGH (70%) power for 1 minute; STIR. If pieces retain some of their original shape, microwave at additional 10- to 15-second intervals, stirring just until melted. Add *remaining* dark chocolate and stir until melted. Spread chocolate into 10×8-inch rectangle on prepared baking sheet.

MICROWAVE white morsels in small, *heavy-duty* plastic food storage bag on MEDIUM-HIGH (70%) power for 30 seconds. Knead bag until morsels are smooth. Add vegetable oil; knead to combine. Cut tiny corner from bag; squeeze to drizzle over dark chocolate. Immediately sprinkle chopped cookies over bark.

REFRIGERATE for 30 minutes or until firm. Break bark into 24 pieces. Store in airtight container at room temperature for up to 1 week.

Jelly Bean Easter Bark

Makes 11 servings (1 pound)

2 cups (12-ounce package)
NESTLÉ® TOLL HOUSE®
Premier White Morsels

2 teaspoons vegetable
shortening

½ cup WONKA® SweeTARTS®
Jelly Beans, *divided*

LINE baking sheet with wax paper.

MICROWAVE morsels and vegetable shortening in medium, uncovered, microwave-safe bowl on MEDIUM-HIGH (70%) power for 1 minute; STIR. Morsels may retain some of their original shape. If necessary, microwave at additional 10- to 15-second intervals, stirring just until morsels are melted. Stir in ¼ cup SweeTarts Jelly Beans.

SPREAD mixture to ¼-inch thickness on prepared baking sheet. Sprinkle with *remaining ¼ cup* SweeTARTS Jelly Beans. Refrigerate for about 15 minutes or until firm. Break into pieces. Store in airtight container at room temperature.

Holiday Peppermint Bark

Makes 15 pieces candy (1 pound)

2 cups (12-ounce package) NESTLÉ® TOLL HOUSE® Premier White Morsels

24 hard peppermint candies, unwrapped

LINE baking sheet with wax paper.

MICROWAVE morsels in medium, uncovered, microwave-safe bowl on MEDIUM-HIGH (70%) power for 1 minute; STIR. Morsels may retain some of their original shape. If necessary, microwave at additional 10- to 15-second intervals, stirring just until morsels are melted.

PLACE peppermint candies in *heavy-duty* plastic bag. Crush candies using rolling pin or other heavy object. While holding strainer over melted morsels, pour crushed candy into strainer. Shake to release all small candy pieces; reserve larger candy pieces. Stir morsel-peppermint mixture.

SPREAD mixture to desired thickness on prepared baking sheet. Sprinkle with reserved candy pieces; press in lightly. Let stand for about 1 hour or until firm. Break into pieces. Store in airtight container at room temperature.

Oatmeal-Chip Cookie Mix in a Jar

Makes about 2 dozen cookies

⅔ **cup all-purpose flour**

½ **teaspoon baking soda**

½ **teaspoon ground cinnamon**

¼ **teaspoon salt**

⅓ **cup packed brown sugar**

⅓ **cup granulated sugar**

¾ **cup NESTLÉ® TOLL HOUSE® Semi-Sweet Chocolate or Butterscotch Flavored Morsels**

1½ **cups quick or old-fashioned oats**

½ **cup chopped nuts**

COMBINE flour, baking soda, cinnamon and salt in small bowl. Place flour mixture in 1-quart jar. Layer remaining ingredients in order listed, pressing lightly after each layer. Seal with lid and decorate with fabric and ribbon.

Recipe to Attach: BEAT ½ cup (1 stick) softened butter or margarine, 1 large egg and ½ teaspoon vanilla extract in large mixer bowl until blended. Add cookie mix; mix well, breaking up any clumps. Drop by rounded tablespoon onto ungreased baking sheets. Bake in preheated 375° F oven for 8 to 10 minutes. Cool on baking sheets for 2 minutes; remove to wire racks. Makes about 2 dozen cookies.

Double Chocolate Warm Pudding Cake

Makes 9 servings

Nonstick cooking spray

1 **cup all-purpose flour**

1¼ **cups granulated sugar,** *divided*

3 **tablespoons** *plus* ¼ **cup NESTLÉ® TOLL HOUSE® Baking Cocoa,** *divided*

2 **teaspoons baking powder**

¼ **teaspoon salt**

1 **can (12 fluid ounces) NESTLÉ® CARNATION® Evaporated Lowfat 2% Milk,** *divided*

1 **tablespoon vegetable oil**

1 **teaspoon vanilla extract**

2 **tablespoons water**

Lowfat whipped topping or ice cream (optional)

PREHEAT oven to 350° F. Spray 8-inch-square baking pan or dish with nonstick cooking spray.

COMBINE flour, *¾ cup* sugar, *3 tablespoons* cocoa, baking powder and salt in medium bowl. Add *½ cup* evaporated milk, vegetable oil and vanilla extract; whisk until just blended. Spread batter into prepared baking pan.

COMBINE *remaining ½ cup* sugar and *¼ cup* cocoa in small bowl. Microwave *remaining 1 cup* evaporated milk and water in small, uncovered, microwave-safe bowl on HIGH (100%) power for 1 minute. Whisk sugar-cocoa mixture into milk mixture until blended. Gently pour over chocolate batter in pan.

BAKE for 20 to 25 minutes (25 to 30 minutes if using glass dish) or until cake layer forms on top and edges are bubbly. Let stand for 10 minutes. Spoon into serving dishes, spooning chocolate sauce over cake. Top with whipped topping.

Tip:

Individual servings can be reheated in microwave for 10 seconds.

Chunky Pecan Pie Bars

Makes 3 dozen bars

CRUST

- 1½ cups all-purpose flour
- ½ cup (1 stick) butter or margarine, softened
- ¼ cup packed brown sugar

FILLING

- 3 large eggs
- ¾ cup corn syrup
- ¾ cup granulated sugar
- 2 tablespoons butter or margarine, melted
- 1 teaspoon vanilla extract
- 1¾ cups (11.5-ounce package) NESTLÉ® TOLL HOUSE® Semi-Sweet Chocolate Chunks
- 1½ cups pecans, coarsely chopped

PREHEAT oven to 350° F. Grease 13×9-inch baking pan.

FOR CRUST

BEAT flour, butter and brown sugar in small mixer bowl until crumbly. Press into prepared baking pan.

BAKE for 12 to 15 minutes or until lightly browned.

FOR FILLING

BEAT eggs, corn syrup, granulated sugar, butter and vanilla extract in medium bowl with wire whisk. Stir in chunks and nuts. Pour evenly over baked crust.

BAKE for 25 to 30 minutes or until set. Cool completely in pan on wire rack. Cut into bars.

Chocolate Indulgence Holiday Gifting Sauce

Makes 16 servings
(2 tablespoons per serving)

2 cups (12-ounce package) NESTLÉ® TOLL HOUSE® Semi-Sweet Chocolate Morsels*

1 cup heavy whipping cream

2 tablespoons light corn syrup

2 to 3 tablespoons flavored liqueur *or* ½ teaspoon flavored extract (optional)

May substitute 1¾ cups (11.5-ounce package) NESTLÉ® TOLL HOUSE® Milk Chocolate Morsels for the Semi-Sweet Chocolate Morsels.

COMBINE morsels, cream and corn syrup in large microwave-safe bowl.

MICROWAVE, uncovered, on HIGH (100%) power for 1 minute; STIR. If necessary, microwave at additional 20- to 30-second intervals, stirring until morsels are melted and sauce is smooth. Add liqueur or extract; mix well.

SERVE warm as a dipping sauce for fresh fruit or spoon over ice cream or cake. Store remaining sauce tightly covered in refrigerator. Makes about 2 cups.

For Gifting: TRANSFER sauce to clean gifting jars; seal well. Refrigerate up to 7 days.

Serving Suggestion:

Serve with sliced pears and seasonal holiday fruits.

Chocolate Chip Cookie Mix in a Jar

1¾ **cups all-purpose flour**

¾ **teaspoon baking soda**

¾ **teaspoon salt**

1½ **cups (9 ounces) NESTLÉ®**
TOLL HOUSE® Semi-Sweet
Chocolate Morsels

¾ **cup packed brown sugar**

½ **cup granulated sugar**

COMBINE flour, baking soda and salt in small bowl. Place flour mixture in 1-quart jar. Layer remaining ingredients in order listed, pressing firmly after each layer. Seal with lid and decorate with fabric and ribbon.

Recipe to Attach: PREHEAT oven to 375° F. **BEAT** ¾ cup (1½ sticks) softened butter or margarine, 1 large egg and ¾ teaspoon vanilla extract in large mixer bowl until blended. Add cookie mix and ½ cup chopped nuts (optional); mix well, breaking up any clumps. Drop by rounded tablespoon onto ungreased baking sheets. **BAKE** for 9 to 11 minutes or until golden brown. Cool on baking sheets for 2 minutes; remove to wire racks to cool completely. Makes about 2 dozen cookies.

Hot Cocoa Mix in a Jar

6 cups NESTLÉ® CARNATION® Instant Nonfat Dry Milk

1½ cups granulated sugar

1 cup plus 2 tablespoons NESTLÉ® TOLL HOUSE® Baking Cocoa

1½ cups miniature marshmallows (optional)

COMBINE dry milk, sugar, cocoa and marshmallows in large bowl. Pour into 2-quart jar or tall container. Seal with lid and decorate with fabric and ribbon.

Recipe to Attach: MEASURE ½ cup cocoa mix into mug. **STIR** in 1 cup hot water or milk. Makes 12 servings.

Variation Using Pint Jar:
1½ cups NESTLÉ® CARNATION® Nonfat Dry Milk
⅓ cup granulated sugar
¼ cup plus 2 tablespoons NESTLÉ® TOLL HOUSE® Baking Cocoa
½ cup miniature marshmallows (optional)

Recipe to Attach: MEASURE ½ cup cocoa mix into mug. **STIR** in 1 cup hot water or milk. Makes 4 servings.

Summer Berry Brownie Torte

Makes 8 to 10 servings

BROWNIE

1	cup granulated sugar, *divided*
6	tablespoons butter or margarine
1	tablespoon water
1½	cups (9 ounces) NESTLÉ® TOLL HOUSE® Semi-Sweet Chocolate Morsels, *divided*
½	teaspoon vanilla extract
2	large eggs
⅔	cup all-purpose flour
¼	teaspoon baking soda
¼	teaspoon salt

FILLING

½	cup heavy whipping cream
2	cups sliced strawberries or other fresh berries

FOR BROWNIE

PREHEAT oven to 350° F. Line 9-inch-round cake pan with wax paper; grease paper.

COMBINE ¾ *cup* sugar, butter and water in small, *heavy-duty* saucepan. Bring to a boil, stirring constantly; remove from heat. Add ¾ *cup* morsels; stir until smooth. Stir in vanilla extract. Add eggs, one at a time, stirring well after each addition. Add flour, baking soda and salt; stir until well blended. Stir in *remaining* morsels. Pour into prepared cake pan.

BAKE for 20 to 25 minutes or until wooden pick inserted in center comes out slightly sticky. Cool in pan for 15 minutes. Invert onto wire rack; remove wax paper. Turn right side up; cool completely.

FOR FILLING

BEAT cream and *remaining* sugar in small mixer bowl until stiff peaks form.

SPREAD filling over brownie; top with berries. Refrigerate until ready to serve.

No-Bake Desserts

No need to turn on the oven with these cool no-bake desserts! Just whip up a simple recipe like Easy No-Bake Crunchy Cranberry Almond Bars for a yummy snack or the Decadent Chocolate Satin Pie for a sweet ending to a nice meal.

Decadent Chocolate Satin Pie

Makes 8 servings

- 1 *prepared* 9-inch (6 ounces) graham cracker crust
- 1¼ cups NESTLÉ® CARNATION® Evaporated Milk
- 2 large egg yolks
- 1⅔ cups (10-ounce package) NESTLÉ® TOLL HOUSE® Dark Chocolate Morsels
- Sweetened whipped cream
- Chopped nuts (optional)

WHISK together evaporated milk and egg yolks in medium saucepan. Heat over medium-low heat, stirring constantly, until mixture is very hot and thickens slightly. Do not boil. Place morsels in food processor fitted with metal blade. With processor running, slowly pour milk mixture into chocolate. Process 10 to 20 seconds. Scrape down sides and continue processing until smooth.

POUR into crust. Refrigerate for 3 hours or until firm. Top with sweetened whipped cream before serving; sprinkle with nuts.

Candy Bars

1⅔ cups (11-ounce package) **NESTLÉ® TOLL HOUSE® Butterscotch Flavored Morsels**

4 cups **toasted rice cereal**

2 packages (11.5 ounces *each*) **NESTLÉ® TOLL HOUSE® Milk Chocolate Morsels, *divided***

GREASE 13×9-inch baking pan.

MICROWAVE butterscotch morsels in large, microwave-safe bowl on MEDIUM-HIGH (70%) power for 1 minute; STIR. Microwave at additional 10- to 20-second intervals, stirring until smooth. Stir in cereal and *1 cup* milk chocolate morsels. Press evenly into prepared baking pan.

MICROWAVE *remaining* milk chocolate morsels in small, microwave-safe bowl on MEDIUM-HIGH (70%) power for 1 minute; STIR. Microwave at additional 10- to 20-second intervals, stirring until smooth. Spread evenly over mixture in pan. Refrigerate until firm. Cut into bars.

No-Bake Dark Chocolate & Mint Cheesecake

1 **prepared 9-inch (6 ounces) chocolate crumb crust**

1⅔ **cups (10-ounce package) NESTLÉ® TOLL HOUSE® Dark Chocolate & Mint Morsels**

2 **packages (8 ounces *each*) ⅓ less fat cream cheese (Neufchâtel), at room temperature**

¾ **cup packed brown sugar**

¼ **cup granulated sugar**

¼ **cup heavy whipping cream, *divided***

1 **teaspoon vanilla extract**

SET aside ½ *cup* morsels for ganache topping. From remaining morsels, sort out *1 tablespoon* mint morsels and place in small, *heavy-duty* plastic bag for drizzle; set aside.

MELT *remaining* morsels in medium, uncovered, microwave-safe bowl on MEDIUM-HIGH (70%) power for 1 minute; STIR. Morsels may retain some of their original shape. If necessary, microwave at additional 10- to 15-second intervals, stirring just until morsels are melted. Cool slightly.

BEAT cream cheese, brown sugar, granulated sugar, *2 tablespoons* cream and vanilla extract in medium mixer bowl on medium speed for 2 minutes. Add melted chocolate; continue beating for 1 minute. Spoon into crust and smooth top.

MICROWAVE *remaining 2 tablespoons* cream in 1-cup glass measure on HIGH (100%) power for 20 seconds or until boiling. Add *reserved ½ cup* morsels to cream; let sit for 1 minute. Stir until smooth. Cool for 5 minutes. Spread ganache over cheesecake to within ¼-inch of edge.

MICROWAVE *reserved* mint morsels in bag on MEDIUM-HIGH (70%) power for 20 seconds; knead. Microwave at 10- to 15-second intervals, kneading until smooth. Cut tiny corner from bag. Drizzle over top of ganache. Refrigerate for at least 2 hours.

Easy No-Bake Crunchy Cranberry Almond Bars

Makes 2 dozen bars

Nonstick cooking spray

4 **cups miniature marshmallows**

¼ **cup (½ stick) butter**

¼ **teaspoon salt**

2 **cups (12-ounce package) NESTLÉ® TOLL HOUSE® Premier White Morsels, divided**

4 **cups toasted wheat cereal squares**

¾ **cup sweetened dried cranberries**

¾ **cup sliced almonds, toasted***

*Note: To toast almonds, bake at 350° F until light golden brown, about 8 minutes, stirring frequently.

LINE 13×9-inch baking pan with foil leaving an overhang on two sides. Spray foil with nonstick cooking spray.

HEAT marshmallows, butter and salt in large, *heavy-duty* saucepan over medium-low heat, stirring frequently, for 5 to 10 minutes, until smooth. Remove from heat. Add *1 cup* morsels; stir until melted.

WORKING QUICKLY, stir in cereal, cranberries, almonds and *remaining 1 cup* morsels. Spread mixture into prepared baking pan with greased spatula, pressing down lightly. Cool for 2 hours or until set. Lift from pan; peel off foil. Cut into bars with serrated knife.

Dark Chocolate & Basil Truffles

Makes 18 servings (2 pieces per serving)

½ **cup heavy whipping cream**

2 **bars (8 ounces) NESTLÉ® TOLL HOUSE® Dark Chocolate Baking Bar**

1 **tablespoon sour cream**

1 **teaspoon light corn syrup**

½ **teaspoon vanilla extract**

3 **tablespoons loosely packed fresh basil leaves (washed and patted dry), finely chopped**

NESTLÉ® TOLL HOUSE® Baking Cocoa

LINE baking sheet with parchment or wax paper.

HEAT cream to a gentle boil in small, *heavy-duty* saucepan. Remove from heat. Add chocolate. Stir until mixture is smooth and chocolate is melted. Add sour cream, corn syrup, vanilla extract and basil; stir to combine. Refrigerate for 15 to 20 minutes or until slightly thickened.

DROP chocolate mixture by rounded measuring teaspoon onto prepared baking sheet. Refrigerate for 1 hour. Shape or roll into balls. Dust truffles with cocoa.* Store in airtight container in refrigerator for up to 3 days. Makes about 3 dozen truffles.

*To dust the truffles, place cocoa in a small, fish mesh strainer and tap over the rolled truffles.

Dark Chocolate Dipped Strawberries & Snacks

Makes 1 cup dip

1⅔ cups (10-ounce package) **NESTLÉ® TOLL HOUSE® Dark Chocolate Morsels**

1 tablespoon vegetable shortening

Fresh strawberries (rinsed and patted dry), pretzels, rippled potato chips and/or cookies*

Assorted sprinkles, finely chopped nuts (optional)

*Assorted bite-size fresh fruit rinsed and patted dry, dried fruit, large marshmallows, cut-up pound cake and nuts can also be used for dipping.

LINE baking sheets with wax paper.

MICROWAVE morsels and vegetable shortening in medium, uncovered, microwave-safe bowl on MEDIUM-HIGH (70%) power for 45 seconds; STIR. Morsels may retain some of their original shape. If necessary, microwave at additional 10- to 15-second intervals, stirring just until morsels are melted.

DIP strawberries (by stem or leaves) or snacks into melted chocolate, tilting bowl to easily dip. Use side of bowl to remove excess. Place on prepared baking sheets. If you are using sprinkles or nuts, sprinkle them on when the chocolate is still wet. Refrigerate for 15 minutes or until set. Makes 1 cup coating.

Creamy Chocolate Pudding

Makes about 4 servings (½-cup per serving)

6 **tablespoons granulated sugar**

¼ **cup NESTLÉ® TOLL HOUSE® Baking Cocoa**

¼ **cup cornstarch**

⅛ **teaspoon salt**

1 **can (12 fluid ounces) NESTLÉ® CARNATION® Evaporated Fat Free Milk**

½ **cup water**

1 **tablespoon butter or margarine**

½ **teaspoon vanilla extract**

COMBINE sugar, cocoa, cornstarch and salt in medium saucepan. Add evaporated milk and water; whisk to blend.

COOK over medium heat, stirring constantly, for about 7 minutes or until pudding thickens (do not boil). Remove from heat; stir in butter and vanilla extract.

Blizzard Party Mix

Makes 8 servings

2 **cups oven-toasted cereal squares**

2 **cups small pretzel twists**

1 **cup dry-roasted peanuts**

1 **cup (about 20) coarsely chopped caramels**

2 **cups (12-ounce package) NESTLÉ® TOLL HOUSE® Premier White Morsels**

SPRAY 13×9-inch baking pan with nonstick cooking spray.

COMBINE cereal, pretzels, peanuts and caramels in large bowl.

MICROWAVE morsels in medium, uncovered microwave-safe bowl on MEDIUM-HIGH (70%) power for 1 minute; STIR. Morsels may retain some of their original shape. If necessary, microwave at additional 10- to 15-second intervals, stirring until smooth. Pour over cereal mixture; stir to coat evenly.

SPREAD mixture into prepared baking pan; let stand for 20 to 30 minutes or until firm. Break into bite-size pieces.

Creamy Chocolate Pudding

Lavender Chocolate Fudge

Makes 4 dozen pieces

⅔ cup (5 fluid-ounce can) NESTLÉ® CARNATION® Evaporated Milk

1 tablespoon dried culinary lavender (use less if desired)

1½ cups granulated sugar

2 tablespoons butter or margarine

¼ teaspoon salt

2 cups miniature marshmallows

1½ cups (9 ounces) NESTLÉ® TOLL HOUSE® Semi-Sweet Chocolate Morsels

1 teaspoon vanilla extract

LINE 8-inch-square baking pan with foil.

PLACE evaporated milk and lavender in medium, microwave-safe bowl. Heat on HIGH (100%) power for 1 minute. Cover with plastic wrap; steep for 10 minutes. Strain into medium, *heavy-duty* saucepan; discard lavender. Add sugar, butter and salt to saucepan; bring to a *full rolling boil* over medium heat, stirring constantly. Boil, stirring constantly, for 4 to 5 minutes. Remove from heat.

ADD marshmallows; stir vigorously until almost melted. Stir in morsels and vanilla extract until melted. Pour into prepared baking pan; refrigerate for 2 hours or until firm. Lift from pan; remove foil. Cut into 48 pieces.

No-Bake Chocolate Cheesecake Pie

Makes 10 servings

1 *prepared* 9-inch (6 ounces) chocolate crumb crust

2 packages (8 ounces *each*) cream cheese, softened

¾ cup packed brown sugar

¼ cup granulated sugar

2 tablespoons milk

1 teaspoon vanilla extract

2 bars (8 ounces) NESTLÉ® TOLL HOUSE® Semi-Sweet Chocolate Baking Bar, melted per label directions and cooled

Sweetened whipped cream (optional)

BEAT cream cheese, brown sugar, granulated sugar, milk and vanilla extract in small mixer bowl on high speed for 2 minutes. Add melted chocolate; beat on medium speed for 2 minutes.

SPOON into crust. Refrigerate for 1½ hours or until firm. Top with whipped cream, if desired.

No-Bake Chocolate Peanut Butter Bars

Makes 5 dozen bars

2 cups peanut butter, *divided*

**¾ cup (1½ sticks) butter,
  softened**

2 cups powdered sugar, *divided*

3 cups graham cracker crumbs

**2 cups (12-ounce package)
  NESTLÉ® TOLL HOUSE®
  Semi-Sweet Chocolate
  Mini Morsels,** *divided*

GREASE 13×9-inch baking pan.

BEAT *1¼ cups* peanut butter and butter in large mixer bowl until creamy. Gradually beat in *1 cup* powdered sugar. With hands or wooden spoon, work in *remaining 1 cup* powdered sugar, graham cracker crumbs and *½ cup* morsels. Press evenly into prepared pan. Smooth top with spatula.

MELT *remaining ¾ cup* peanut butter and *remaining 1½ cups* morsels in medium, *heavy-duty* saucepan over *lowest* possible heat, stirring constantly, until smooth. Spread over graham cracker crust in pan. Refrigerate for at least 1 hour or until chocolate is firm; cut into bars. Store in covered container in refrigerator.

Chocolate Dipped Caramels with Sea Salt

Makes 25 candies

1 cup (6 ounces) NESTLÉ®
  TOLL HOUSE® Semi-Sweet
  Chocolate Morsels

1 teaspoon vegetable
  shortening

1 package (5.5 ounces) about
  25 pieces, soft & chewy
  rectangular caramels,*
  unwrapped

⅛ to ¼ teaspoon coarse sea salt

*25 square caramels can be substituted for the
rectangular caramels.

LINE baking sheet with wax paper.

MICROWAVE morsels and vegetable shortening in small, uncovered, microwave-safe bowl on HIGH (100%) power for 1 minute; STIR. Morsels may retain some of their original shape. If necessary, microwave at additional 10- to 15-second intervals, stirring just until morsels are melted; cool slightly.

DIP caramel pieces, using a fork, into melted chocolate. Shake off or scrape excess chocolate against side of bowl. Place on prepared baking sheet. Sprinkle with sea salt. Refrigerate for 15 minutes or until set.

Notes:

● 1 cup (6 ounces) NESTLÉ® TOLL HOUSE® Milk Chocolate Morsels can be substituted for the Semi-Sweet Chocolate Morsels. Melt milk chocolate morsels at MEDIUM-HIGH (70%) power.

● Amount of candies made may vary pending size of caramels used. If there is any melted chocolate remaining after dipping caramels, try dipping pretzels or potato chips!

Creamy Crunchy Haystacks

Makes 40 candies

2 cups (12-ounce package) **NESTLÉ® TOLL HOUSE® Premier White Morsels**

1 tablespoon vegetable shortening

1 cup pretzel sticks, broken into 1-inch pieces

1 cup almond slivers, toasted

½ cup unsweetened or sweetened flaked coconut, toasted

MICROWAVE morsels and vegetable shortening in large, uncovered, microwave-safe bowl on MEDIUM-HIGH (70%) for 1 minute; STIR. Morsels may retain some of their original shape. If necessary, microwave at additional 10- to 15-second intervals, stirring just until morsels are melted. Stir in pretzel sticks, almonds and coconut; toss until all ingredients are coated. Drop by level tablespoon onto prepared trays. Refrigerate for 30 minutes. Store in tightly covered container.

Double Boiler Method: COMBINE pretzel sticks, almonds and coconut in large bowl. Place morsels and shortening in top of double boiler over hot (not boiling) water. Do not cover. When most of the morsels are shiny, stir just until melted. (Prevent water from coming in contact with morsels.) Remove from heat. Pour melted morsels over pretzel mixture; toss until all ingredients are coated. Proceed as above.

Peanut Butter Crunchy Haystacks: SUBSTITUTE ¾ cup creamy or crunchy peanut butter for the vegetable shortening. Proceed as above.

Tip:

If you do not have on hand or a preference for pretzel sticks, almonds and/or coconut, try using granola, popcorn, toasted rice cereal, pecans, macadamia nuts, peanuts, pistachios and/or crumbled shredded wheat cereal instead.

Dark Chocolate Bark

Makes 9 servings

½ cup broken mini pretzel
    twists

½ cup coarsely broken rippled
    potato chips

¼ cup coarsely chopped lightly
    salted peanuts

1⅔ cups (10-ounce package)
    NESTLÉ® TOLL HOUSE®
    Dark Chocolate Morsels

LINE baking sheet with wax paper.

COMBINE pretzels, chips and peanuts in small bowl.

MICROWAVE morsels in small, uncovered, microwave-safe bowl on MEDIUM-HIGH (70%) power for 45 seconds; STIR. If pieces retain some of their original shape, microwave at additional 10- to 15-second intervals, stirring just until melted. Stir in *half* of snack-pretzel mixture.

POUR onto prepared baking sheet. Spread mixture to desired thickness. Sprinkle with *remaining* snack-pretzel mixture. Tap sheet several times to spread chocolate and settle pretzels. Refrigerate for 30 minutes or until firm. Break into pieces. Store in airtight container at room temperature. Best when eaten within 24 hours.

Impress Your Guests

Be the hit at every party with delicious cakes, pies, and more from Nestlé! Whether it's chocolate, cheesecake, peanut butter, or something a little more fruity, these flavors are sure to leave your guests asking for seconds.

Chocolate Mudslide Frozen Pie

Makes 8 servings

- 1 *prepared* 9-inch (6 ounces) chocolate crumb crust
- 1 cup (6 ounces) NESTLÉ® TOLL HOUSE® Semi-Sweet Chocolate Morsels
- 1 teaspoon NESCAFÉ® TASTER'S CHOICE® House Blend 100% Pure Instant Coffee Granules
- 1 teaspoon hot water
- ¾ cup sour cream
- ½ cup granulated sugar
- 1 teaspoon vanilla extract
- 1½ cups heavy whipping cream
- 1 cup powdered sugar
- ¼ cup NESTLÉ® TOLL HOUSE® Baking Cocoa
- 2 tablespoons NESTLÉ® TOLL HOUSE® Semi-Sweet Chocolate Mini Morsels

MELT 1 cup morsels in small, *heavy-duty* saucepan over *lowest possible* heat. When morsels begin to melt, remove from heat; stir. Return to heat for a few seconds at a time, stirring until smooth. Remove from heat; cool for 10 minutes.

COMBINE coffee granules and water in medium bowl. Add sour cream, granulated sugar and vanilla extract; stir until sugar is dissolved. Stir in melted chocolate until smooth. Spread into crust; refrigerate.

BEAT cream, powdered sugar and cocoa in small mixer bowl until stiff peaks form. Spread or pipe over chocolate layer. Sprinkle with mini morsels. Freeze for at least 6 hours or until firm.

Dark Chocolate Ganache Brownie Cakes

Makes 15 servings

DARK CHOCOLATE BROWNIE CAKES

- 1⅔ cups (10 ounces) NESTLÉ® TOLL HOUSE® Dark Chocolate Morsels
- 1½ cups granulated sugar
- ½ cup (1 stick) unsalted butter, cut into pieces
- 3 tablespoons water
- 3 large eggs
- 1½ teaspoons vanilla extract
- 1 cup plus 2 tablespoons all-purpose flour
- ¼ teaspoon salt
- 2½-inch round metal cookie cutter

DARK CHOCOLATE GANACHE

- ½ cup heavy whipping cream
- 1 cup (6 ounces) NESTLÉ® TOLL HOUSE® Dark Chocolate Morsels

FOR DARK CHOCOLATE BROWNIE CAKES

PREHEAT oven to 325° F. Line 13×9-inch baking pan with foil; lightly grease.

HEAT morsels, sugar, butter and water in medium saucepan over low heat, stirring constantly, until chocolate and butter are melted. Remove from heat. Stir in eggs, one at a time, until blended. Stir in vanilla extract. Add flour and salt; stir well. Pour into prepared baking pan.

BAKE for 30 to 35 minutes or until wooden pick inserted in center comes out slightly sticky. Cool completely in pan on wire rack. Holding sides of foil, lift brownie from pan to cutting board. Carefully remove foil and return brownie to board. Cut away ¼-inch from each side. Cut out 15 cakes with cookie cutter, twisting gently to remove. For easier cutting, cutter can be wiped clean and/or greased lightly between cuttings. Scraps can be saved for another use, such as an ice cream topping, milkshakes or a snack. Serve cakes with Dark Chocolate Ganache.

FOR DARK CHOCOLATE GANACHE

HEAT cream in 2-cup microwave-safe glass measure or small bowl on HIGH (100%) power for 30 to 40 seconds. Slowly add morsels. Cover with plastic wrap and let stand for 5 minutes. Stir well. Refrigerate any remaining ganache. Makes 1 cup.

Tips:

- ½ cup NESTLÉ® CARNATION® Evaporated Milk can be substituted for the heavy whipping cream.

- Cake squares can be made instead of cake rounds. After cutting edges from brownie, cut into 20 squares.

Turtle Cheesecake

Makes 12 to 16 servings

CRUST

- 1¾ cups chocolate graham cracker crumbs
- ⅓ cup butter or margarine, melted

FILLING

- 3 packages (8 ounces *each*) cream cheese, softened
- 1 can (14 ounces) NESTLÉ® CARNATION® Sweetened Condensed Milk
- ½ cup granulated sugar
- 3 large eggs
- 3 tablespoons lime juice
- 1 tablespoon vanilla extract
- 1½ cups (9 ounces) NESTLÉ® TOLL HOUSE® Semi-Sweet Chocolate Morsels
- 2 tablespoons NESTLÉ® NESQUIK® Chocolate Flavor Syrup
- 2 tablespoons caramel syrup or ice cream topping
- ½ cup coarsely chopped pecans
- ¼ cup NESTLÉ® TOLL HOUSE® Semi-Sweet Chocolate Mini Morsels

PREHEAT oven to 300° F. Grease 9-inch springform pan.

FOR CRUST

COMBINE crumbs and butter in medium bowl. Press onto bottom and 1 inch up side of prepared pan.

FOR FILLING

BEAT cream cheese and sweetened condensed milk in large mixer bowl until smooth. Add sugar, eggs, lime juice and vanilla extract; beat until combined.

MICROWAVE 1½ cups morsels in medium, uncovered, microwave-safe bowl on HIGH (100%) power for 1 minute; STIR. Morsels may retain some of their original shape. If necessary, microwave at additional 10- to 15-second intervals, stirring just until morsels are melted. Stir 2 cups of cheesecake batter into melted morsels; mix well. Alternately spoon batters into crust, beginning and ending with yellow batter.

BAKE for 70 to 75 minutes or until edge is set and center moves slightly. Cool in pan on wire rack for 10 minutes; run knife around edge of cheesecake. Cool completely. Drizzle Nesquik and caramel syrup over cheesecake. Sprinkle with pecans and mini morsels. Refrigerate for several hours or overnight. Remove side of pan.

Rich Chocolate Cake with Peanut Butter Milk Chocolate Frosting

Makes 12 servings

CAKE

- **2 cups all-purpose flour**
- **1¾ cups granulated sugar**
- **⅔ cup NESTLÉ® TOLL HOUSE® Baking Cocoa**
- **1½ teaspoons baking powder**
- **1½ teaspoons baking soda**
- **½ teaspoon salt**
- **1 cup milk**
- **1 cup water**
- **½ cup vegetable oil**
- **2 large eggs**
- **2 teaspoons vanilla extract**
- **1⅔ cups (11-ounce package) NESTLÉ® TOLL HOUSE® Peanut Butter & Milk Chocolate Morsels, *divided***

CREAMY PEANUT BUTTER MILK CHOCOLATE FROSTING

- **1 package (8 ounces) cream cheese, softened**
- **1 teaspoon vanilla extract**
- **⅛ teaspoon salt**
- **3 cups powdered sugar**

FOR CAKE

PREHEAT oven to 350° F. Grease and flour two 9-inch-round cake pans.

COMBINE flour, granulated sugar, cocoa, baking powder, baking soda and salt in large mixer bowl. Add milk, water, vegetable oil, eggs and vanilla extract; blend until moistened. Beat for 2 minutes (batter will be thin). Pour into prepared pans. Sprinkle *⅓ cup* morsels over each cake layer.

BAKE for 25 to 30 minutes or until wooden pick inserted in center comes out clean. Cool in pans on wire racks for 10 minutes; remove to wire racks to cool completely. Frost with Creamy Peanut Butter Milk Chocolate Frosting.

FOR CREAMY PEANUT BUTTER MILK CHOCOLATE FROSTING

MICROWAVE *remaining* morsels in small, uncovered, microwave-safe bowl on MEDIUM-HIGH (70%) power for 1 minute; STIR. Morsels may retain some of their original shape. If necessary, microwave at additional 10- to 15-second intervals, stirring just until morsels are melted. Beat cream cheese, melted morsels, vanilla extract and salt in small mixer bowl until light and fluffy. Gradually beat in powdered sugar.

Mocha Dream Cake

CAKE

- 1½ cups hot water
- 1 tablespoon NESCAFÉ® TASTER'S CHOICE® House Blend 100% Pure Instant Coffee Granules
- 1 cup original NESTLÉ® COFFEE-MATE® Powdered Coffee Creamer
- 2⅓ cups all-purpose flour, *divided*
- 1½ teaspoons baking soda
- 1⅓ cups (8 ounces) NESTLÉ® TOLL HOUSE® Premier White Morsels
- ⅓ cup vegetable oil
- 1⅔ cups granulated sugar
- 4 large eggs
- ⅔ cup (5 fluid-ounce can) NESTLÉ® CARNATION® Evaporated Milk
- 2 tablespoons white vinegar
- 1 teaspoon vanilla extract
- ⅔ cup NESTLÉ® TOLL HOUSE® Baking Cocoa

FROSTING

- ⅔ cup NESTLÉ® TOLL HOUSE® Premier White Morsels
- ⅓ cup butter or margarine
- 1½ teaspoons water
- 1 tablespoon NESCAFÉ® TASTER'S CHOICE® House Blend 100% Pure Instant Coffee Granules
- 2 packages (3 ounces *each*) cream cheese, softened
- 4 to 4½ cups powdered sugar

PREHEAT oven to 350° F. Grease and flour two 9-inch-round cake pans.

FOR CAKE

COMBINE water and coffee granules in medium bowl. Stir in Coffee-mate with wire whisk. Combine *1⅔ cups* flour and baking soda in another medium bowl.

MICROWAVE 1⅓ cups morsels and vegetable oil in large, uncovered, microwave-safe bowl on MEDIUM-HIGH (70%) power for 1 minute; STIR. Morsels may retain some of their original shape. If necessary, microwave at additional 10- to 15-second intervals, stirring just until melted. Add coffee mixture, sugar, eggs, evaporated milk, vinegar and vanilla extract to melted morsels; mix with wire whisk. Gradually beat in flour mixture until combined. (Batter will be thin.) Pour *3¼ cups* batter into medium bowl; stir in *remaining* flour. Pour into prepared pans.

BLEND cocoa into *remaining* batter with wire whisk until blended. Slowly pour even amounts of cocoa batter into center of each pan. (Cocoa batter will spread evenly outward from center.)

BAKE for 40 to 45 minutes or until wooden pick inserted in center comes out clean. Cool in pans on wire racks for 10 minutes; remove to wire racks to cool completely. Frost cake with frosting between layers and on top and side of cake.

FOR FROSTING

MICROWAVE ⅔ cup morsels and butter in large, uncovered, microwave-safe bowl on MEDIUM-HIGH (70%) power for 1 minute; STIR. Morsels may retain some of their original shape. If necessary, microwave at additional 10- to 15-second intervals, stirring just until melted. Combine water and coffee granules in small bowl. Beat cream cheese and coffee mixture into melted morsels. Gradually beat in powdered sugar until mixture reaches spreading consistency. Makes about 2½ cups.

Premier White Lemony Cheesecake

CRUST

- **6 tablespoons butter or margarine, softened**
- **¼ cup granulated sugar**
- **1¼ cups all-purpose flour**
- **1 large egg yolk**
- **⅛ teaspoon salt**

FILLING

- **3 bars (12 ounces) NESTLÉ® TOLL HOUSE® Premier White Baking Bar,* broken into pieces**
- **½ cup heavy whipping cream**
- **2 packages (8 ounces *each*) cream cheese, softened**
- **1 tablespoon lemon juice**
- **2 teaspoons grated lemon peel**
- **¼ teaspoon salt**
- **3 large egg whites**
- **1 large egg**

May use 2 cups (12-ounce package) NESTLÉ® TOLL HOUSE® Premier White Morsels instead of baking bars.

PREHEAT oven to 350° F. Lightly grease 9-inch springform pan.

FOR CRUST

BEAT butter and sugar in small mixer bowl until creamy. Beat in flour, egg yolk and salt. Press mixture onto bottom and 1 inch up side of prepared pan.

BAKE for 14 to 16 minutes or until crust is set.

FOR FILLING

MICROWAVE baking bars and cream in medium, uncovered, microwave-safe bowl on MEDIUM-HIGH (70%) power for 1 minute; STIR. Morsels may retain some of their original shape. If necessary, microwave at additional 10- to 15-second intervals, stirring just until melted.

BEAT cream cheese, lemon juice, lemon peel and salt in large mixer bowl until smooth. Gradually beat in melted baking bars. Beat in egg whites and whole egg. Pour into crust.

BAKE for 35 to 40 minutes or until edge is lightly browned. Run knife around edge of cheesecake. Cool completely in pan on wire rack. Refrigerate for several hours or overnight. Remove side of springform pan. Garnish as desired.

Doubly Decadent Dark Chocolate Cheesecake

Makes 16 servings

1⅔ cups (10-ounce package)
   NESTLÉ® TOLL HOUSE®
   Dark Chocolate Morsels,
   divided

1½ cups graham cracker crumbs

 1 cup plus 2 tablespoons
   granulated sugar, *divided*

¼ cup (½ stick) butter, melted

 3 packages (8 ounces each)
   cream cheese, softened

½ cup sour cream

 1 teaspoon vanilla extract

 3 large eggs

⅓ cup heavy whipping cream

PREHEAT oven to 350° F. Tightly wrap outside bottom and side of 9-inch springform pan with two pieces of foil to prevent leakage.

MICROWAVE *1¼ cups* morsels in small, uncovered, microwave-safe bowl on MEDIUM-HIGH (70%) power for 1 minute; STIR. Morsels may retain some of their original shape. If necessary, microwave at additional 10- to 15-second intervals, stirring just until smooth. Cool to room temperature.

COMBINE crumbs, *2 tablespoons* granulated sugar and butter in ungreased 9-inch springform pan. Press onto bottom and 1 inch up side of pan.

BEAT cream cheese, *remaining 1 cup* sugar, sour cream and vanilla extract in large mixer bowl until creamy. Add eggs, one at a time, beating well after each addition. Beat in melted chocolate until blended. Pour onto crust. Place pan in large roasting pan; fill roasting pan with hot water to 1-inch depth.

BAKE for 45 to 50 minutes or until edges are set but center still moves slightly. Remove cheesecake from water bath to wire rack. Run wet knife around edge of cheesecake. Refrigerate for 1 hour and remove side of pan.

MICROWAVE *remaining* morsels and whipping cream in small, uncovered, microwave-safe bowl on MEDIUM-HIGH (70%) power for 1 to 2 minutes; STIR. Morsels may retain some of their original shape. If necessary, microwave at additional 10- to 15-second intervals, stirring just until smooth; cool for 5 minutes. Spread over cheesecake. Refrigerate for 4 hours or overnight.

Chocolate Peanut Butter Tart

Makes 12 servings

CRUST

- 1½ **cups all-purpose flour**
- ¼ **cup plus 1 tablespoon finely chopped peanuts, *divided***
- ¼ **cup granulated sugar**
- 10 **tablespoons butter, melted**

  Nonstick cooking spray

GANACHE

- 1¼ **cups heavy whipping cream**
- 2 **cups (12-ounce package) NESTLE® TOLL HOUSE® Semi-Sweet Chocolate Morsels**
- 2 **tablespoons butter, softened**

FILLING

- 1 **cup creamy peanut butter**
- 2 **tablespoons powdered sugar**

FOR CRUST

PREHEAT oven to 400° F.

COMBINE flour, ¼ *cup* peanuts, granulated sugar and butter in medium bowl. Press dough evenly onto bottom and side of ungreased 9- to 10-inch tart pan with removable bottom. Spray 10-inch piece of foil with nonstick cooking spray. Gently press oiled side down on top of dough. Using a fork, poke holes through foil and crust to create air vents.

BAKE for 15 minutes; remove foil. Continue baking for an additional 5 to 10 minutes or until edges are golden brown and bottom of crust is baked. Cool completely in pan on wire rack.

FOR GANACHE

HEAT cream in medium, *heavy-duty* saucepan over low heat, stirring occasionally until it just comes to a boil. Remove from heat. Stir in morsels and butter. Let stand for 3 minutes. Stir until mixture is smooth. Refrigerate for 20 minutes.

FOR FILLING

COMBINE peanut butter and powdered sugar in small bowl.

TO ASSEMBLE

SPOON peanut butter filling onto bottom of prepared crust and spread evenly. Pour ganache on top. Gently tap the pan on the counter to create a smooth surface. Sprinkle surface with *remaining 1 tablespoon* of chopped peanuts. Refrigerate for 3 hours or until firm. Cut into slices and serve.

Chocolate Truffle Cake with Strawberry Sauce

Makes 12 servings

TRUFFLE CAKE

- 1¾ cups (11.5-ounce package) NESTLÉ® TOLL HOUSE® Milk Chocolate Morsels, *divided*
- ½ cup (1 stick) butter
- 3 large eggs
- ⅔ cup granulated sugar
- 1 teaspoon vanilla extract
- ¼ teaspoon salt
- ⅔ cup all-purpose flour

GLAZE

- ¼ cup NESTLÉ® TOLL HOUSE® Butterscotch Flavored Morsels
- ¼ cup creamy peanut butter

SAUCE

- 2 cups fresh or frozen strawberries, thawed
- 2 tablespoons granulated sugar

  Garnish suggestions: whipped topping, fresh strawberries, mint leaves

FOR TRUFFLE CAKE

PREHEAT oven to 350° F. Grease and flour 9-inch springform pan. Melt *1 cup* milk chocolate morsels and butter in small, uncovered, microwave-safe bowl on MEDIUM-HIGH (70%) power for 1 minute; STIR. Morsels may retain some of their original shape. If necessary, microwave at additional 10- to 15-second intervals, stirring just until melted. Cool for 10 minutes.

BEAT eggs, ⅔ cup sugar, vanilla extract and salt in large mixer bowl. Blend in chocolate mixture. Stir in flour; mix well. Pour into prepared pan.

BAKE for 30 to 35 minutes or until wooden pick inserted in center comes out clean. Cool completely in pan on wire rack. Remove side of pan.

FOR GLAZE

MELT *remaining* milk chocolate morsels, butterscotch morsels and peanut butter in small, uncovered, microwave-safe bowl on MEDIUM-HIGH (70%) power for 1 minute; STIR. Morsels may retain some of their original shape. If necessary, microwave at additional 10- to 15-second intervals, stirring just until melted. Cool slightly. Spread glaze over top and sides of cooled cake. Refrigerate for 30 minutes or until glaze is set.

FOR SAUCE

PLACE strawberries and 2 tablespoons sugar in blender; cover. Blend until smooth. Refrigerate until serving time. To serve, cut into wedges. Garnish with strawberry sauce, whipped topping, strawberries and mint leaves.

Sensational S'more Torte

TORTE

- 1¾ **cups all-purpose flour**
- 1¾ **cups granulated sugar**
- ¾ **cup NESTLÉ® TOLL HOUSE® Baking Cocoa**
- 1½ **teaspoons baking soda**
- 1 **teaspoon salt**
- 1½ **cups sour cream**
- ⅔ **cup butter, softened**
- 2 **large eggs**
- 1½ **teaspoons vanilla extract**

FILLING

- 2 **cups (12-ounce package) NESTLÉ® TOLL HOUSE® Semi-Sweet Chocolate Mini Morsels**
- 1 **package (3.5 ounces) vanilla instant pudding and pie filling mix**
- 1 **cup cold milk**
- 1 **package (8 ounces) cream cheese, softened**
- 1 **container (12 ounces) frozen whipped topping, thawed**
- 4 **cups miniature marshmallows, *divided***
- 16 **whole graham crackers**
- 10 **fudge-covered graham crackers or 5 squares chocolate graham crackers**

FOR TORTE

PREHEAT oven to 350° F. Grease and line bottom of two 8-inch-square cake pans with parchment paper.

COMBINE flour, sugar, baking cocoa, baking soda and salt in large mixer bowl. Beat in sour cream, butter, eggs and vanilla extract until just moistened. Beat on medium speed for 3 to 4 minutes or until light in color. Spoon into prepared pans.

BAKE for 40 to 45 minutes or until wooden pick inserted in center comes out clean. Cool in pans on wire racks for 10 minutes; remove to wire racks to cool completely.

FOR FILLING

MICROWAVE morsels in microwave-safe bowl on HIGH (100%) power for 1 minute; STIR. Morsels may retain some of their original shape. If necessary, microwave at additional 10- to 15-second intervals, stirring just until smooth.

COMBINE pudding mix and milk in large mixer bowl. Beat for 2 minutes or until thickened. Beat in cream cheese. Fold in whipped topping. Fold in *3 cups* marshmallows.

SLICE each cake layer in half horizontally. Place two layers, side-by-side, cut-side-down on large serving platter. Spread half the melted chocolate over the cake layers. Lightly press half the graham crackers into melted chocolate, cutting crackers to fit. Spread half the filling over graham crackers. Repeat with *remaining* cake layers, melted chocolate, graham crackers and filling, covering tops only, not sides of cake.

COARSELY CHOP chocolate covered graham crackers. Sprinkle over top of torte. Sprinkle with *remaining* marshmallows. Refrigerate for at least 5 hours or overnight.

Incredible Banana Split Cake

Makes 12 to 16 servings

½ cup (1 stick) butter

2 large eggs

2¾ cups all-purpose flour

2½ teaspoons baking powder

1 teaspoon salt

1 can (15¼ ounces) pineapple tidbits in juice, undrained

½ cup buttermilk

1¼ cups (7.5 ounces) granulated sugar

⅔ cup mashed banana

1 teaspoon vanilla extract

1¼ cups NESTLÉ® TOLL HOUSE® Semi-Sweet Chocolate Morsels

½ cup chopped walnuts, toasted, *divided*

1½ cups chopped fresh strawberries

1 cup chopped banana

Chocolate Glaze (recipe follows)

ALLOW butter and eggs to stand at room temperature for 30 minutes. Grease and lightly flour a 12-cup Bundt pan.

PREHEAT oven to 350° F.

COMBINE flour, baking powder and salt in medium bowl. Drain pineapple tidbits, reserving ¼ *cup* juice. Combine *reserved* pineapple juice and buttermilk in small bowl.

BEAT butter in large mixer bowl on medium to high speed for 30 seconds. Gradually add sugar, ¼ cup at a time, beating on medium speed until well combined. Add eggs, mashed banana and vanilla extract; beat well. Alternately add flour mixture and buttermilk mixture, beating on low speed after each addition just until combined. Stir in morsels and ¼ *cup* walnuts. Gently fold in drained pineapple tidbits, strawberries and banana. Spread batter into prepared pan.

BAKE for 60 to 65 minutes or until a wooden pick inserted near center comes out clean. Cool cake in pan on wire rack for 20 minutes. Remove from pan; cool completely on wire rack. Drizzle cake with Chocolate Glaze and sprinkle with *remaining ¼ cup* walnuts. Cover; refrigerate at least 2 hours before serving.

Chocolate Glaze: **HEAT** ¾ cup NESTLÉ® TOLL HOUSE® Semi-Sweet Chocolate Morsels, 3 tablespoons butter and 3 tablespoons light corn syrup in small saucepan over low heat, stirring until chocolate melts and mixture is smooth. Use immediately.

Gimme S'More Pie

1   **can (12 fluid ounces) NESTLÉ® CARNATION® Evaporated Milk,** *divided*

1   **package (3.9 ounces) chocolate instant pudding and pie filling mix**

1   *prepared* **9-inch (6 ounces) graham cracker crumb crust**

3   **cups mini marshmallows,** *divided*

2   **cups frozen whipped topping, thawed**

½   **cup NESTLÉ® TOLL HOUSE® Milk Chocolate Morsels**

WHISK *1¼ cups* evaporated milk and pudding mix in medium bowl until well blended. Pour into crust.

MICROWAVE *2 cups* marshmallows and *remaining ¼ cup* evaporated milk in medium, uncovered, microwave-safe bowl on HIGH (100%) power for 30 to 45 seconds; stir until smooth. Let stand for 15 minutes. Gently fold in whipped topping. Spoon marshmallow mixture over chocolate layer; smooth top with spatula.

REFRIGERATE for 2 hours or until set. Top with *remaining 1 cup* marshmallows and morsels.

Tip:

For a gooey S'more topping, place chilled pie on a baking sheet. Preheat broiler. Place baking sheet with pie on rack 6 inches from broiler unit (pie top should be at least 4 inches from broiler unit). Broil for 30 seconds or until marshmallows are light brown and morsels are shiny. Watch carefully as browning occurs very fast! A handheld kitchen butane torch can be used as well.

Butterscotch Pecan Perfection Pie

1 *unbaked* 9-inch (4-cup volume) deep-dish pie shell*

1⅔ cups (11-ounce package) NESTLÉ® TOLL HOUSE® Butterscotch Flavored Morsels, *divided*

¾ cup light corn syrup

3 large eggs, at room temperature

1 tablespoon all-purpose flour

¼ teaspoon salt

1½ cups pecan halves, coarsely chopped

1½ cups whipped cream (optional)

If using frozen pie shell, use deep-dish style. Do not thaw. Bake on baking sheet.

PREHEAT oven to 350° F.

MELT *1⅓ cups* morsels in medium, uncovered, microwave-safe bowl on MEDIUM-HIGH (70%) power for 1 minute; STIR. Morsels may retain some of their original shape. If necessary, microwave at additional 10- to 15-second intervals, stirring just until melted.

ADD corn syrup, eggs, flour and salt to melted morsels. Beat on medium until smooth. Stir in pecans. Pour pecan mixture into pie shell.

BAKE for 40 to 45 minutes or until knife inserted into center comes out with little bits of filling attached. If browning too quickly, cover with foil. Cool on wire rack for 2 hours. Refrigerate 1 hour or until serving time.

TO GARNISH AND SERVE

LINE baking sheet with wax paper.

PLACE *remaining* morsels in *heavy-duty* plastic bag. Microwave on MEDIUM-HIGH (70%) power for 30 to 45 seconds; knead. Microwave at 10- to 15-second intervals, kneading until smooth. Cut tiny corner from bag. Drizzle 10 circular designs about 2 inches high and wide onto prepared baking sheet. Refrigerate for 5 to 10 minutes or until firm.

PLACE 10 dollops of whipped cream around edge of pie. Remove drizzle designs from refrigerator. With tip of knife, gently remove designs from wax paper and insert, standing up, into dollops. Serve immediately.

Variation:

⅓ cup NESTLÉ® TOLL HOUSE® Semi-Sweet Chocolate Morsels can also be melted and made into drizzle designs instead of the Butterscotch Flavored Morsels.

Tip:

Two shallow (2-cup volume) pie shells can be substituted for the one deep-dish pie shell. Follow directions above and bake for 30 to 35 minutes.

Chocolate Lover's Chocolate Mousse Pie

Makes 12 servings

1 cup graham cracker crumbs

⅓ cup NESTLÉ® TOLL HOUSE® Baking Cocoa

¼ cup granulated sugar

⅓ cup butter, melted

2¼ cups (16 ounces) NESTLÉ® TOLL HOUSE® Semi-Sweet Chocolate Morsels, *divided*

2 cups heavy whipping cream, *divided*

2 teaspoons powdered sugar

1 teaspoon vanilla extract

PREHEAT oven to 350° F.

COMBINE graham cracker crumbs, cocoa and granulated sugar in 9-inch pie plate. Stir in butter until moistened; press onto bottom and up sides of pie plate.

BAKE for 8 to 10 minutes. Sprinkle *½ cup* morsels over bottom of hot crust; let stand for 10 minutes or until all morsels are shiny. Spread chocolate over bottom and up side of crust. Cool to room temperature.

MICROWAVE *2 cups* morsels and ¾ *cup* cream in large, uncovered, microwave-safe bowl on HIGH (100%) power for 1 minute; STIR. The morsels may retain some of their original shape. If necessary, microwave at additional 10- to 15-second intervals, stirring just until morsels are melted. Cool to room temperature.

BEAT *remaining* cream, powdered sugar and vanilla extract in chilled small mixer bowl until soft peaks form. Fold 2 cups whipped cream into chocolate mixture. Spoon into crust; swirl top. Garnish with *remaining* whipped cream. Refrigerate until firm.

MICROWAVE *remaining ¼ cup* morsels in *heavy-duty* plastic bag on HIGH (100%) power for about 30 seconds; knead until smooth. Cut tiny corner from bag; squeeze to drizzle chocolate over pie. Let stand a few minutes before serving.

INDEX